SOY CHINGONA

BREAKING BARRIERS: A WOMAN'S PATH TO SUCCESS

PAOLA GARCIA

Paola Garcia
Soy Chingona: Breaking Barriers A Woman's Path To Success

All rights reserved
Copyright © 2023 by Paola Garcia

Published by Spines
ISBN: 979-8-89383-397-3

ACKNOWLEDGMENTS

This book is to inspire others who might feel different to embrace it. We only have one life, so let's make the best version of it. Please don't let a disability stop you from going after your dreams. I want to thank my true close friends; they have been there supporting my dreams no matter what. Thank you also to my TikTok family; in a way, they helped me heal, and without their constant support, I wouldn't be here. I wouldn't be here if it wasn't for my parents; they sacrificed many things, and their support made me the woman I am now.

Mama y Papa, gracias por todo y ojalá que todo mi trabajo que he hecho los haga orgullosos de la hija y la mujer en que me he convertido.

1

———————

A little girl full of life and dreams for a world that was not prepared for her uniqueness to stand out. Hi, I'm Paola I was born with Cerebral Palsy which affected my motor skills and slightly my speech. As a little girl, I was not aware that having a disability was a big deal to the rest of the world. My story starts on August 20, 1992, when I was born. I was like any other baby until I was 3 months old when my parents noticed I would not grab my bottle with my hands and kept them close most of the time. At 6 months old I finally got diagnosed with Cerebral Palsy, but the doctors did not take the time to explain what exactly CP was and how it was going to affect me in my daily life as I grew up. Also, the doctors didn't inform my parents that Cerebral Palsy was something I would have all my life. Unfortunately, there is no cure for CP, but my parents assumed that as I grew up it would go away. The doctors not only failed to inform my parents about how CP would affect me but also about the type of Cerebral Palsy I had. Cerebral Palsy is not genetic as many assume, but is caused by a lack of oxygen to the brain. Mine was caused by a lack of oxygen during labor and delivery. Many call me lucky due to the fact my CP turned out so severe as many cases. I used to question why was I lucky, lucky to have Cerebral Palsy. I grew older and understood why.

The very first traumatic event I experienced was at 3 years old. Cerebral palsy causes your muscles to be so tied. I was beginning to walk by being held by my hands and my parents noticed I would walk on my tippy toes. They took me to the doctor and my parents were informed this was common in individuals with CP. The doctor told my parents surgery ASAP before my muscles got more tied. At just 3 years old went into a long surgery. I remember bits and pieces. I remember screaming for my mom and getting poked so many times. The recovery from this surgery was three long months. I put in a cast from my waist down to my toes. Now I look at the scars on my legs I don't get them anymore because I think the muscles on my legs would have gotten so much worse without surgery.

Fast forward 5 years later, my parents decided to move to Mexico without being aware of how this move would affect me in good ways and bad ways. My grandpa my dad's father was diagnosed with cancer and my dad wanted to expend the time my grandpa had left before he passed away. When we moved to Mexico right away my parents tried to register me in school to start kindergarten. I realised my older brother started school fast, but I did not. As time passed, I would ask my mom, "Ma, ¿cuándo voy a ir a la escuela también?" and my mom would always responded with, "Mija, ya pronto." After 5 months of living in Mexico, my mom told me I was starting school. The day came when I went to my new school and it was not what I expected. I was excited to learn to read, write, and count but that did not happen. The type of school I was registered in was more of a daycare type of center for kids with disabilities.

Little Paola quickly realised this school was not going to be it. I felt unhappy going to school every day. From a very young age, I was always eager to learn new things. The entire aspect of school learning to read, count, and write made me excited. The teachers at this so-called "school" would not teach us anything they only did physical therapy and I remember all I wanted was to learn how to write like my cousins and older brother. Yes, all the physical therapy I received at this school helped so much with my muscles being so tied. I was tired of every single day just getting physical therapy. So, I finally asked my mom why they put me in that school she said "Mija, es que aquí no aceptan niñas como tu en escuela regulares."

Basically, schools in Mexico do not accept kids with disabilities in regular classrooms and that was the first time I remember being mad for being "different." I constantly begged my parents to switch schools and I would only get "ahorita no se puede" or "tienes que esperar", that's when I started questioning why I had to be different or why others had a problem with me being "different". Also, this is when a man came into my "school" looking for girls to be in his show and he picked me. I was already 6 years old and did not know how to read one single word so how was I supposed to learn my lines? My mom Rosa came to the rescue she would read my lines to me every day and I would repeat them. At that moment discovered I could learn more so I would point to random words I would see on the street and ask my mom to read them and that's how I learned to read and spell. I was chosen to be in this show I did not think it was a big deal until I found out we were performing in one of the biggest theatres in Culiacan. I had the lead performance and at this time I still could not walk by myself, so you may ask then how would you plan on performing on a stage where you need to be standing and walking? Well, the producer found me a walker I could use and this walker was so unique because it was like a horse I did not have to use my hands to use it since I had difficulty holding things. For a little girl that did not know how to read I memorised my lines and as well as the rest of the cast. The show was a big success and that helped me realise being different was not that bad and I can be creative to do things I want. After this my parents started looking at different schools I could go to. My parents got a call from a school to take me so I could take a test. My parents assumed it was a test everyone took to get into the school. Well it was not the case I took the test I scored 100 percent, yet I was not accepted. The principal said, "Your daughter is very smart but kids like that do not learn and parents do not feel comfortable having their kids around kids like your daughter." I remember asking my parents why I could not go if I passed and if I was not going to do anything to the other kids.

For the next year, I took different tests at multiple schools to get in. I passed every single test but I was not accepted because of my disability. This is when I experienced discrimination for the first time just because I was "different" did not mean I was not capable of learning. After an entire year of not getting accepted into a school. Finally, I got into the most unexpected school I could think of. The elementary school I got accepted to was in the very outside of the city in the countryside. It was a developing school meaning the school had minimal things because it was located in a poor community. My first day of actual school was finally hear I was starting first grade at age 8 when I was supposed to be in third grade. When I was in my classroom sitting at my desk I felt so much happiness and the sense that this was where I belonged. Unfortunately, this did not last long because my parents decided after the school ended we were moving back to California. I could not leave Mexico without leaving a mark.

School testing came along and there was a rumor from the school district that with these tests they were going to prove that kids with disabilities cannot learn and just take a space in the classroom. I remember clearly the day of testing I showed up to an empty classroom and I overheard one of the school districts say, "La pusimos sola para que no le copie a nadie, a ver cómo le va." Basically, I was put alone from the rest so I would not copy because to them that was the only way I was going to pass. When I heard that I got this feeling inside of me of anger with empowerment to prove them wrong. The day of the results from the testing was here and I was not worried. My name got called last because I not only had the highest score in my classroom but from the entire school. The shock on the principal face was epic I smiled and said to myself "That's how you do it."

2

I was a very resourceful girl. I always found ways to do things like walking. I was about to be 9 years old and I still did not walk on my own, but that did not stop me from being mobile. I used the feeding chair to push around, the stroller, and anything I could push around. The doctors would always tell my parents I would walk when I was ready and they were right. The day before were left Mexico I just started walking on my own.

After of few weeks of adjustment to being back in California it was time to go back to school. My 9-year-old self was not prepared for the countless years of bullying she was about to face. I started 3rd grade at Wilcox Elementary School in Montebello California. I was assigned a TA who was like a teacher's assistant, but just to help me write since I can't use my hands and help me during lunch. I was never going to forget these two TA's names because they impacted my life in good and bad ways. Martha my TA was bilingual since I was barely learning English it would help me with the language barrier. So that is what I thought the school district thought, but she became the biggest bully I had at Wilcox Elementary.

Three months into attending 3rd grade, I had made good friends with Sofia, Marisol, and Gaby since day one they did not see me as different at all I was like everyone else. My teacher Mrs. Gonzales would treat me like the rest of her students and I loved it. Mrs. Gonzales would be asked, "Can someone raise their hand and tell me a verb?" I raised my hand to say, "Walk." Mrs. Gonzales answered, "Good job Paola, can you now read the full sentence?" I followed to read the sentence: "The boy walk to the store."

This entire time I could see my TA Martha's face being so serious more like angry that I got the answer correct. This went on for weeks her attitude changed she was so serious and angry towards me for anything. I did not tell anyone because I did not want to be a bother. One day Martha's true colours came out and I will never forget this day because it was one of many times she humiliated me in front of my classmates.

Every month we had an activity we had to complete I got one section wrong because I was still learning English. It was about to be our first recess of the day and Martha told me, "You're not allowed to go to recess because you got all this section wrong." I told her, "But why if I was not the only one that got it wrong and they going to recess." "You not going to recess because I say you're not until you learn to read correctly. I stayed quiet but in my mind, I was like why are you yelling at me? I clearly remember my eyes started to fill up with tears. Mrs. Gonzales was not in the room when this happened and at that moment I did not think anything about it but I felt so embarrassed getting yelled at in front of my classmates. Martha proceeded to put the packet in front of me but aggressively that I felt scared she was going to hit me. Martha told me, "Paola are you so dumb that you don't know how to sound out the words?" I told her, "I'm trying but I don't know what you want from me" Martha slapped my deck yelling, "You are a dumb girl, girls like you don't learn you are wasting my time" At this moment I lost it I start crying because I was scared of her. Once recess was over Miss Gonzales saw me there "Oh Paola why didn't you go to recess?" before I could answer her Martha told her, "Oh she didn't want to she not feeling good." I froze because was scared of Martha and if I told Mrs. Gonzales that was not true she was not going to believe me. Martha kept me from going to my recess for weeks my fear kept growing because I would see in her eyes how angry she would get and she would also enjoy making me cry. Until one I was so scared of going to school that I started faking that I did not feel good so I could stay home. It worked for a couple of days until my mom realised I was just saying to stay home. The little girl who was so eager to attend school had turned her excitement into fear. My mom asked me, "¿Qué pasa? ¿Por qué no quieres ir a la escuela?" She wanted to know what was going on. I told her what Martha was doing to me. She told me, "Mija yo voy hablar a la escuela." The next she went to talk to the principal and while I was in class Martha got called to the principal office. Martha returned and I could see the anger on her face and I was scared. Recess came around I was prepared for her to make me stay in the classroom, but Mrs. Gonzales approached me "Paola you can go to recess Mrs. Evans is going to go with you." I can only see how the anger on Martha's face towards me grew.

The humiliations Martha did to me did not stop, they

just decreased for some time. Mrs. Evans became my part-time TA and loved it. She was the best. She would let me be me and saw that I was learning all the material not how Martha made it seem. 3rd grade came to an end and I was all set for 4th grade in my mind I thought after the multiple complaints there were about Martha the school district would change my TA for the new school year. My surprise Martha was in my 4th grade classroom. She had this smirk on her face when she saw my reaction seeing her there like, "Jaja, you thought you were getting rid of me!" I was scared but at the same time, I was not going to let her do whatever she liked with me.

Fourth grade was going great my teacher Mrs. Figueroa was amazing. I loved school but Martha's anger towards me grew because I did not let her negatively get me anymore. Martha humiliated me one more time and she knew how to do it when nobody was around because it would be my word against mine. School year testing came around and a part of the testing had to do with writing a mini essay. The school made accommodations for me to use a computer to type my essay. Martha was over my shoulder just looking and I was given extra time to finish. Everyone left and I was alone Martha took this opportunity to tell me, "You are doing everything wrong, you don't know how to write. You are so dumb!" The unexpected happened and Martha pulled my hair; the fear traveled to my body and I froze. Martha was holding my hair and telling me, "If you say anything I could do worse things." "You are going to start all over and you're not going to lunch." The fear I felt was unexplainable and my 9-year-old self did her best to hold her tears back.

Mrs. Evans and Mrs. Figueroa came in and were still in

shock I wanted to cry but in my mind, I was like, "I'm not going to give you the pleasure of seeing my cry." Both Mrs. Figueroa and Evans told me I could go to lunch and that I could finish after. Mrs. Evans could tell something happened "Paola are you okay? Did Martha do something? I said, "No I'm just tired." She knew I was not going to do anything. Martha came and Mrs. Evans proceeded to cover my ears and told something to Martha. I was scared that Martha would pull my hair again or try to hit me, so for the rest of the school year, I did whatever she said.

The fourth-grade camp was getting close and Martha had told me I was not allowed to go because I was going to be a bother to everyone and that the school did not want me to go. At that moment I felt anger because I thought the reason why I was not being allowed to was due to me being "different." I went home and told my parents "I hate being different. It's not fair I get left out of doing things." My mom asked, "¿Por qué dices eso?" I told her what Martha had told and she said she was going to find out if it was true. The next morning it was like any other morning bus drop off except Martha was not there to pick me up Mrs. Figueroa was and I was happy because that meant Martha was not working that day, or so I thought. Mrs. Figueroa asked me, "Paola who told you you aren't allowed to go to 4th grade camp?" "Martha told me," I told her, and remember her smiling at me and saying, "That's not true Paola we absolutely want you to come Martha had the wrong information they are talking to her right now," I remember being happy because I was going to 4th grade camp but scared at the same time because Martha did come to work and she was going to mad I told on her. Martha did not waste time to let me know how angry she was with me she left me without lunch that day. I was not surprised she was doing this because it was not the first time she had denied me from lunch, so I smiled and went on with my day like nothing and it made her angrier.

3

It was the first day of 5th grade new school, new teacher, and new classmates and I was nervous not due to the new environment I was going to be in, but because I did not want Martha to be my TA again. At the bus drop-off at Montebello Middle School, I did not see Martha and the relief I felt was unbelievable. I was a little nervous because I did not know who my new TA was, but I thought to myself "It can't be worse than Martha." I was taken to my 5th-grade classroom and a new TA was there Marisela. "Paola nice to meet you I'm super excited to work with you, you tell me what you need me to help you" I smiled and was happy because it was not Martha, but mostly she seemed nice and friendly. I was assigned to Mr. Garcia's classroom and the cool part I had my good friends Sofia and Marisol with me in the same class. 5th grade school year finally felt like a normal school year.

School was great and at home, things started to change. We were living at my aunt's house Tere and we weren't the only ones living there. A house of three bedrooms 9 people were living there. We had a bedroom for us where all five of us slept and had our stuff. As kids we liked to play, when my aunt was home we weren't allowed to play or make noise because she would get mad. We started not to like her being home because everything would bother her. My parents started looking for a house to buy in the area for us to move to, but unfortunately, my parents could not afford it. Things started getting more complicated at home and my brothers and I could tell. My brothers and I got to a point where we slept on an inflatable mattress in the living because the room was already super crowded. This situation went on for a year until we took a trip to the valley to visit my mom's family. My dad liked the area and started looking at houses. One day my parents pulled me out of school and this wasn't normal so went I got in the car I asked them, "¿Qué pasa? ¿A dónde vamos?" My dad responded with "A firmar los papeles de la casa." Even when he told me were going to go sign the papers for the house it still didn't hit me that we were moving 5 hours away from everything I knew.

4

On October 11, 2004, I moved to Atwater California. I had a month that I started 7th grade and I had to move to not only a new town but a new school. I was really sad because I finally was comfortable, fitted in, and had amazing friends and I had to leave to start all over again. A week after moving it was time to register me to my new middle school and I was so nervous. We get to the school office and right away I feel all eyes on me and I overhear "What are going to do? We never had someone like her here..." All I could think was "Here we go again." I was scared that I was not going to be allowed to go to school. My mom explained that was not the case the school district just needed time to find a TA and prepare the teachers because I would be the first student with a disability who could attend a normal classroom.

The district school called after a few days I was set to start school the next day. My first day at Mitchell Senior Middle School was here and I was nervous because I was going to be the new girl but the "different" new girl. I knew everyone was going to stare at me and I didn't like it. At this age, it started to bother me that people would stare because I was "different." I arrived at school and my TA Ashely was there. I was a little upset because the bus was super late to pick me up and I arrived at school in the middle of the first period, I was like, "Great I'm walking into the middle of class and everyone going to stare at me even more." They going to be "Who's that in a wheelchair? She's weird." I was not looking forward to the stares but we were about to go in. I went in and just like I thought everyone was staring and wouldn't stop staring. Ashely handed the papers to the teacher and she pointed to my seat. As I took my seat my English teacher introduced me to the class and after that, my classmates stopped staring at me.

Since the periods at Mitchell Senior were longer than LA we got a little break between periods. I was planning on staying inside the classroom, but a group of girls invited me to go outside with them. Greta, Evelyn, and Mariela were the first not only to talk to me, but they didn't look at me differently. After this I was less nervous because I was making friends, my teachers were great and my TA was a cool person.

I was settling in good at my new house and school but things were about to change. I started to get bullied at school by the "popular" girl and I started having a crush on a boy in my English class. I was making friends everyone knew who I was and that's what Melissa didn't like. Honestly, I didn't want to be the "popular" girl and I wasn't it but Melissa thought I was. We had a chat program at school where we could send messages to our classmates. Melissa started sending me messages, "Hey, retarded girl." "You are ugly." I didn't respond but I was upset because I thought I was going to catch a break here from getting bullied. My anger towards myself started to grow because I was different and that's why everyone hated me.

My crush on the boy in my English class grew bigger we started talking through myspace. This was the first boy I talked to wanting it to be more than friends. Melissa found out about my crush and told the entire school through a group chat, so I wanted to disappear that day. I was embarrassed and angry. Every time we ran into each other and saw my TA wasn't with me she would yell, "retard" so everyone would look and most would laugh. During lunch time my TA was not with me because that was her break time as well and that's when Melissa would come over trying to start stuff so I would get suspended I didn't give in, but in my mind, I was like "Just defend yourself, Paola, push her, pull her hair maybe then she would leave you alone." I knew that's what she wanted and I did the opposite I smiled and that made her more mad. I remember going home a lot of the day upset and angry with myself.

THERE WERE nights I waited for my parents to go to bed so I could scream and cry myself to sleep. I would cry at night questioning why I had to be different and why I had to put up with people bullying me. At this age, I was still learning about my disability, and being a teenager itself is a difficult stage in life. This is where you are discovering yourself. Being a teenager plus having a disability was starting to be a bit too overwhelming. I didn't tell my parent or anyone at school what was going on because I just didn't want to bring more attention to myself and I was tired of always being the "problem." The bullying got physical Melissa came up to me during lunch and knew I had difficulty walking tells me, "Hi retard move" I was standing up but I was not going to move. Melissa pulled my hair and pushed me at the same time which made me fall backwards. Melissa and her friends laugh and say "Oops the retard girl fell let's help her," but I got up and walked away. I felt so much anger at that moment I wanted to cry but from anger. I have never felt the urge to hit someone so much as I did at this moment. I wanted to pull Melissa's hair but I controlled myself I tried to play it out so that it didn't bother what just happened, but a lot of people saw what happened. That night was not different in the aspect of crying myself to sleep, but it was the first time the thought of me not living across my mine. The thought of me being dead would be much better I wouldn't be a bother to anyone and I wouldn't be missed.

5

The end of middle school was here I was happy to be graduating and going to high school mostly because Melissa was going to a different high school than I was. I was sad because my TA Ashely was not going to be my TA in high school. I managed to graduate middle school in good spirits regardless of all the bullying I experienced. Summertime was here and I was enjoying not going to school getting called names and getting laughed at. During summer time I was happier with myself and was less angry from being different and hating having a disability.

There were two weeks left of summer vacation and that's when my mom informed me that I wasn't going to have a TA at school. My first thought was "Yesss!" because I wouldn't have to deal with my TA being a bully. Then, my thought was "who going to help me write my notes and class work I don't want to get behind." "I don't have a computer here to do it myself and I can't write with my hands." "Why do I have to be like this?" Quickly the hate I had for my disability came back.

My first day at Atwater High School was here and I was so nervous because staring, and not knowing who was in my classes was hard for me. I arrived at Atwater High and the school psychologist was there waiting for me, Mrs. Garcia. "Hi, Paola come with I'm going to walk with you to your first period and explain the accommodations we made for you." I was preparing myself to meet a new TA and I was scared because what if my new TA be like the one I had in Montebello? We got to her office and there was nobody there, so I was confused. "Paola here we did different accommodations for you to feel more comfortable." They won't be assigned a person as my TA instead in every of my class periods a student from the junior or senior year will be assigned as my TA I was nervous because I would have a different person but at the same time, I was excited because I was going to be around kids my age at all time and I was not going to be the "weird" girl always having an adult following her. I noticed that other kids wouldn't talk to me because I had an adult with me all the time and I used to hate it and blame myself because to me it was my fault I had to have a TA all the time. So now that my TA was a kid from my school I was happy and it meant I wouldn't be the "weird girl" having an adult following her all the time at school. I went to my first period and as I predicted everyone was staring and I didn't know anybody. I can hear all the low talks about me as I get out of my wheelchair to walk to my assigned seat. I was so embarrassed and mad because why did this always have to happen to me? Why can I be normal, I went to my seat pretending I didn't feel the stares on me and I didn't hear the talks about me. My TA for my first period came she was a junior and from the start we got along really well, that's when I felt high school was not going to be so bad after all or that's what I thought. Lunch came along and I was alone and I thought to myself "Yes the weird girl is eating alone with a lady that has to help me eat." I was so mad at myself for needing the help because it brought attention to me that I didn't want. I wanted to make friends, but instead, I wanted to crawl under a rock and never come out. I was upset going to 5th period when I saw him sitting next to my desk I automatically smiled and I wondered who he was because he seemed older to be in my English class. Mrs. B tells me "Paola this is Christian he will be your TA this period." I said "Hi," and he said "Hi" back and smiled. I was happy and I smiled back. He quickly offered to help me get out of my wheelchair but I got it. When we were seated I was nervous to look his way because I didn't want him to notice me smile every time I looked at him. I went to my last period happy, but that didn't last long. The person who would ruin most of my high school years was there. Spanish class was my last period and I was generally happy with taking Spanish. Mitchell didn't lose time making fun of me but made sure I only heard her. I ignore her comments of "weird, alien, gross, and retarted." I went home and my parents asked me how was it and I said, "Muy bien, me gusta mucho." I lied that I loved it because I just didn't want to be more of a bother to them and I will just suck it up. From a very young age, I learn to keep my feelings to myself. For reasons of not being listened to and when I did I was blamed for part of the things that happened to me due to having a disability.

The next day I was just going around campus in my wheelchair killing time and I saw my friends from middle school and finally had people to hang out with during lunch. I was looking forward to the 5th period because I was going to see Christian. He was there before I got to class he smiled when he saw me. 5th period quickly became my favourite period especially since it would take my mind off being the weird girl that everyone stares at. He would make me laugh with jokes and have a conversation with me. I knew I was starting to like him more than just friends but he was a senior and I was like "Paola you're crazy if you think a guy like that is going to like you, especially a senior." As freshman year continued yes 5th period was my escape from getting bullied by Mitchell. I noticed she hated that I was making friends and friends from other grades. Mitchell was smart because she would bully me when I was alone or through MySpace.

I liked to get to my classes on time and PE was my first period. My teacher told me I didn't have to change because she didn't want me to go through more difficulty, but I still had a locker in the locker room to leave my stuff. Mitchell also had PE at the same time and one of many times she spit on my hair on her way out of the locker room. Some laughed and others just looked shocked and embarrassed. You may be asking why I didn't tell my parents or someone in school. The reason was that I didn't want to get more attention and be the "weird girl" who couldn't defend herself. The nights that I would cry myself to sleep started happening more often. My hate towards myself for having a disability started to grow more.

During this time freshman year, my quince was going to happen and I was excited in some ways I wasn't about it. I knew my parents were making a big sacrifice by saving all they could for me to have the best quince party. My chamberlain was going to be my older brother Ramon and I was content with the idea, but at the same time I disliked the idea because I knew others would say "Look her brother had to be her chamberlain because she couldn't get anybody else." The next day I went to my first period which was PE class and I noticed him. His olive-green eyes caught my attention. I asked my TA, "Who is he?" "That's Alex the new TA for the class". I made eye contact but right away I looked away because I didn't want the same thing that happened with Christian where Mitchell made fun of me in front of everyone for my crush on him. I jokingly told my friend Jas, "Omg I like him to be my chamberlan" Jas "Ask him then to be on your quince." I right away told her "You're crazy yeah right he would never say yes he going to think I'm weird" Finally that Friday I decided to ask Alex to be my chambelan but I was so shy to talk to him because I didn't want him to know I had a crush on him.

I decided to write him a note and to this day I remember what the note said:

Hi Alex, this is Paola. I'm having my quince in 2 months.
I like to see if you would like to be my chamberlain.
If yes call me at this number.

I gave the note to Jas to give to Alex because I was too shy to give it to give. Alex opened the note and just smiled but I didn't get a response. I was so embarrassed and stupid for thinking someone as good-looking as Alex was going to be seen dancing with the weird girl from school. I hated myself for trying to be "normal" that night it didn't fail I cried myself to sleep not because I didn't get an answer, but because I hated my disability and that hate kept growing.

The next day I was in my room on myspace when my phone rang. When I answered, a male voice said, "Hi Paola, this is Alex. How are you?" I was in shock he called me and I didn't expect what he was going to tell me next. "Yes, I will be your chamberlain." I was in shock and it took me a minute to answer because I was processing that Alex told me yes. I told him when our next practice was and he told me, "Okay Paola I see you Monday in class." When I hung up I screamed with excitement and the entire weekend I couldn't stop smiling. My happiness didn't last long because Mitchell found out I asked Alex to be my chamberlain and she began to bully me about it. I felt bad for him and embarrassed for him because it was my fault she was spreading rumours. I apologised to him and he said "You don't have to apologise is okay we both know they are just rumours that aren't true and I still want to be your chamberlain."

A few quince practices have passed by and Alex and I are getting along so well and my feelings for him are also growing. One of my favourite days was practice because I got to spend more time with my Friends who were part of my court and Alex. One day after practice Alex pulled me aside because he wanted to ask me something "I want to see what you are doing Friday?" "Nothing.?" I was a little confused as to why he wanted to know what I was doing. Alex asked, "Want to go to the movies?" I was surprised that he was asking me to go to the movies with him on a date. "Yes," I told him I had the biggest smile and I was in shock that the boy I have a crush on asked me on a date like me I was the weird girl.

Friday came along Alex told me he would pick me up and my dad wasn't happy but it wasn't anything new because he hardly let me go out. The reason why my friends wouldn't invite me out was because they knew my parents wouldn't allow me to go. My dad being mad was not going to ruin this for me. I was nervous because I had never been on a date and I didn't know if he liked me like I liked him.

The date went great he told me he liked me and how pretty I was. When I got home I was on cloud nine and we agreed to keep it a secret to avoid Mitchell making rumours. Keeping it a secret was his idea and I didn't think anything bad about it at first. There were a few days left until my quince and every time I tried to approach him at school he would avoid me and Mitchell and her friends would giggle every time. I thought she was doing it just to bother me. I found out that Alex and Mitchell had made a beat that he could make me believe he liked me as a girlfriend. My first thought was Mitchell was lying but I heard them talking. I wanted to crawl into a hole and never get out. There were only 2 days left until my quince and I wanted nothing to do with it especially after I found out about Mitchell's game with Alex. The thought of "I'm just going to be a laughing joke to everyone", but it was too late to cancel. My hate towards myself grew even more and this was the first time I had the thought, "What if I wasn't I lived everything would be better." The thought of not being alive sounded better than being the laughing joke. My quince day was here and I had to fake in front of everyone that I just didn't get heartbroken, but I didn't let this take my happiness away for the most part. I felt happy seeing my family from Mexico was here for my special day. The entire day I tried to avoid Alex as much I could and for my luck, I was sick too. We got to the hall where my party was going to be and to my surprise a girl was waiting for him. His girlfriend. "what?" He had a girlfriend this entire time. I wanted to scream, cry, and run away but instead, I smiled and walked away.

6

———————

After my quince, I completely stop talking to Alex. I didn't let him know I knew his game with Mitchell. I remember being like a zombie at school for days I was there but my mind was somewhere else. Mitchell would make her jokes I just didn't care at this point I just didn't want to be alive. I blame myself and my disability for being the jokes of everyone. At the age of 15, I had so much hate towards myself due to my disability and my high school years got worse. My sophomore year I completely went off the rails. I let my grades slip so much that I flank my math class. All I cared about was to fit in, and feel "normal" like everybody else. I started drinking alcohol because that's what the people I was hanging out with would do. I smoked weed for the first time I was going to be cool like my friends and my relationship with my parents got worse. They didn't understand why I was acting out and had no clue multiple nights I had contemplated ways I could take my life. I hated being alive with a disability nobody was going to like me this way and there was no reason to be alive.

Of course, the bullying against me continued to my junior year of high school. By this point, I had become an expert at faking that I was happy when I was around people, but in reality, I was dying inside. One day my friends asked me to stay with them after school because they were going to a school club and thought it would be a good idea to be all together. I did and to my surprise, Mitchell was one of the leaders of the club. The last thing I wanted to do was spend more time around her. My friends saw my face and told me "Paola stay ignore her." I was taken by surprise, so did they know Mitchell was bullying me, I didn't want to ask them. The after-school club sounded fun and I knew most of the people there. The club lip sync, which meant we would dance and our principal would lip-sign the song. This was a competition of many high schools. The idea started to sound fun until Mitchell said out loud "To be part of this you have to be able to move correctly and dance." I knew that was targeted at me and a lot of the people there knew as well because she was looking at me while she said it. Maybe a few weeks before if she had said this I would have walked away, but for the first time in a long time, I was excited to be part of something despite my disability. I waited until the meeting was over and went to ask my Spanish teacher if he was actually in charge. Mitchell was already talking to him and I didn't care.

"Mr. Gutierrez, is it okay if I join the club?"

"Of course, why you ask?"

"I asked because of my disability and some moves I might do differently"

He said, "Paola don't worry I'm happy you have joined the club you are an example."

I didn't understand at first why he said I was an example.

Mitchell then told him I was going to ruin the routine because I needed certain modifications. The teacher told her, "She's staying and the modification will be made." I smiled and Mitchell was fuming. The practices were going well I felt great about myself and I wasn't letting my disability get in my way of enjoying the high school memories I was making with my friends. One day during practice we were told to give ideas for our performance outfits. I gave my idea and the group liked it because it went with our team, but of course the "leader" Mitchell didn't like it because I came up with it and at this point, my friends noticed what was going on. My idea didn't get picked and I was okay with it, but Mitchell was so happy because she won. I could care less about it and that bothers her. The day of the dancing competition was getting closer and honestly, I was more excited than nervous. I was proud of myself because I was doing the entire dance routine with minimal accommodations. This moment was one of the moments I was happy with myself and I stopped caring what others thought about me. The day of the competition was here and Mitchell pulled me aside before getting on the bus and told me, "Just remember if we loss is all your fault retard." I just laughed and her comments didn't bother me anymore. When we went up stage I couldn't believe I was up there and I gave it my all. In that moment I felt the most alive I have felt in a long time. I was comfortable in my skin. Unfortunately, we didn't place to move on but it was the coolest experience. Yes, Mitchell was upset and blamed me, but honestly, I didn't care. She was not going to take this accomplishment away from me. You might be asking what accomplishment? The accomplishment of doing something I enjoy without letting my disability stop me, being more secure in my skin, embracing my disability, and not caring what others had to say about me.

7

———

Senior year was here finally I was so excited to start senior year. I was more comfortable in my skin and yes I still avoid Mitcheal in school because I wanted to enjoy my senior year with no drama. Michael was angry because her comments wouldn't get to me like they used to. My mindset changed that I don't have to fit in and that's okay. This includes having a boyfriend. In the second week of senior year, most of the girls were going crazy for a new boy that starting in our school. Honestly, I didn't care because I knew he wasn't going to look at me because of my disability or that's what I thought. I went to my AP Spanish class and the new boy was sitting behind me I heard, "Hi, I'm Issac. What's your name?" I was in shock he was talking to me. I said, "Paola nice to meet you." I smiled then he said, "Oye, ¿y aqui sí podemos hablar español, verdad?"

Right off the bat, I got attracted to his accent. So I asked him, "¿Tu, de dónde eres?" He responded, "Soy de Puerto Rico."

I smiled and from the side eye, I could see Micheal just

staring. I minded my own business because I wanted a peaceful senior year and I wanted to focus more on my education because I was thinking of attending college. I always had good grades during my school years, but had always had to work double just to prove to the teachers I was capable of learning the material just like my classmates and I did my work. Of course, I started noticing more my senior year and it motivated me more to do more than my best.

The time started to apply for college finally was here and I started to get comments from everyone that I wasn't going to make it. Even my own family would tell me I was crazy for thinking I could attend college and it was a waste of money. I was hurt to hear that but I didn't let that stop me like other times. Even Issac supported me and we became really good friends. I had a crush on him. I liked him and he saw me by who I was and not by "the weird girl" who had a disability. I kept getting bullied but I learned how not to let it get to me as much as it did before. I stopped questioning why I had to have a disability and be different.

I started to be okay with being "different" and embracing the way I was. I started applying to colleges and applied far from home because I wanted to live that college experience like everybody else. Later on, I realized that was one of the worst decisions I could have made. I received a call from a university informing me that they are interested in me. I was excited because an actual university wanted me. The university was an hour away from my house and my parents started to use my disability as an excuse for why I couldn't attend that university. My mom would constantly ask me, "¿Quién piensas que te va ayudar? Tu sola no puedes." Always reminding me I will need help and nobody will want to help me except her. My mom always reminding me would make me so mad because instead of believing in me, they would always doubt me and blame my disability for why I couldn't do certain things. Yes, I was aware I was going to need help if I moved to college in doing my hair, bathing, and support with dressing. This didn't mean I couldn't do it I just needed to find the correct resources where they support you with this. I tried to get that across to my parents, but to them, it didn't exist and it was something unrealistic. I was getting tired of them always bringing up my disability to things I "wasn't" going to able to do because I have Cerebral Palsy. In my head, I screamed to them "I know have a disability stop reminding me I'm normal." When I tried to express to them what I felt when they would do that I would only get my dad yelling and sometimes telling me if I didn't stop talking he would slap me. I would instead cry in my room and keep questioning "Why had to be like this? Why?" I had more days again that I was angry with myself for having a disability and I didn't want to go back to that because I was embracing my disability it was part of me.

January came along and my friend Jessy told me she had a call for an interview from the same university I received a call from. We both decided to accept the interview and go on the same day. When I told my parents that I accepted the interview they told me "Estás loca, para qué?" I knew they were going to tell me I was crazy for thinking I could go to that college away from home. I honestly didn't care and I was excited because my friend was interested in going to the same college as me. The day of the interview was finally here and yes I was nervous. When we arrived at the university it wasn't what I expected a university to look like. It looked like an ordinary building more of a clinic/office. The building wasn't as big as a university would be. I wasn't sure what to think about it, but I told myself maybe during the interview I would learn more about the school. I checked in and waited to get called for my interview. When I heard my name "Paola Garcia" get called I frost for a second and told myself, "Everything will be okay, you got this."

During the interview the questions weren't hard it was more about how I want to pursue a higher education. After the interview, I did have to take a test to see where my English and Math levels were at. If I passed the test I would be accepted into the university. I took the test I could feel eyes on me the entire time to see if was coming from the other individuals in the testing room. I knew they were observing me because when it was my friend's turn nobody was in the room observing her. The entire situation made me mad because just because I have a disability it doesn't mean I need to copy someone else test to pass. I passed the test and when they told me, "Good job! We are surprised with the scores!" I noticed a tone in her voice of sarcasm and shock that I'm good in school. I was upset because again I had to prove to others I was worth going to college just like everyone else. After this situation, you would think I waited to hear back from other colleges to decide where my best option was. No, I didn't wait I chose to go to that university in Fresno California an hour away. My parents were not happy with my decision and kept telling me I couldn't move. My main reason for choosing this university was because I wanted to get away from home. I still had to make sure I was going to graduate high school. Senior year wasn't turning out to be that bad after all.

I was still crushing on Issac. We would text 24/7 and would walk me to my classes not caring what the others had to say. Mitchell would try everything to get his attention just to get under my skin. I honestly at this point didn't care it was another boy and all I wanted was to be done with high school so I didn't have to see her again. I did senior activities and I was surprised I enjoyed them. Everyone was talking about who their dates were going to be for senior prom. I kept telling myself "Who going to want to be your date, weird girl." The idea of not having a date for prom did bother me a little because of my disability it was something more I wasn't going to be able to do as everyone else. "Another thing Mitchell is going to bully me about," I thought to myself. I started to not want to go to prom and I was getting mad at myself again. Then I overheard a few of my classmates they were going to prom without dates. Hearing them made me realise I could go to prom with my friends even though I didn't have a date. I started to get excited about prom and I went prom dress shopping. Prom was around the corner and in school all it was talked about was who was going to be their date. I didn't want to hear about it because even when I was okay going by myself, deep down I did wish I had a date to share that special memory of senior year. A week before prom Issac was waiting for me at my locker, "Hey can we hang out during lunch? I need to talk to you." "Yes, about what?" Issac smiled and walked away. The entire morning I couldn't concentrate in class because I was thinking about what he wanted to talk about. In my head, I was "What if it's another of Mitchell's games." "He probably wants you to help him with homework." Lunchtime came around and I went to my locker as I always do and Issac was there. I couldn't help but smile. I liked him and he would honestly make my day better at school.

"Hi, what do you want to tell me?"

"Let's go get lunch and I tell you" He had a smile on his

face and I smiled even more. I was taken aback that he wanted to have lunch with me. Out of no where he tells me "te ves muy bonita, como siempre." I blushed and I didn't know how to respond to a boy complimenting me on looking beautiful. I smiled and laughed. He then hugged me and I was really in shock. I felt like he was playing like everyone else does because I'm "the weird" girl everyone sees as a toy to have fun. I was peppering myself for another prank of my classmates.

We grabbed our lunch and went to sit on the outside benches. Finally, he said, "You know how prom is next Saturday, wanted to ask you if you would like to go to prom with me?"

I was in total shock and the only thing that came out of my mouth was, "You are joking right?"

His response was, "Why do you think I'm joking? Is that a no?"

"Because you know I'm the weird that everyone here makes fun of," I told him.

"What you mean 'weird girl'? You are an amazing girl and to me, you are normal like everyone here. *No les hagas caso a los que se burlen de ti, te tienen celos.*"

I was mind-blown when he told me that the ones that bullied me were jealous of me. He honestly cared about my feelings so I gave him the answer to his question. "Yes, I will go to prom with you." I had the biggest smile and kissed me on my cheek. I was screaming in the inside.

Prom night was finally here and Jess came to my house to get ready together. I told Issac to not pick me up because I didn't want to deal with my dad. I was in love with my prom dress. It was a gold dress and my favourite part was the tail. My dad gave us a ride and I wasn't happy about it, but it was the only way I was allowed to go to prom. Issac was already there and he looked so handsome in his suit matching with me.

"Hola. Estás hermosa."

"Muchas gracias, tu te ves muy guapo."

I can't believe I told him that out loud how handsome he looked. Prom Night was one of the best memories I have had from all my high school years. I didn't care how others were looking at me when I was dancing. I enjoy dancing and laughing with my friends. That night I knew Issac liked me the same way I liked him more than just friends. I felt like I was dreaming.

8

Graduation was just a week away and I was ready. Finally free of all the bullying that's all I wanted. I told myself nothing can't be worse, so I thought. Until our last class Mitchell didn't leave me alone she told me, "You are not going to be anybody in life just a retarded girl wanna-be-normal-human. You disgust me." I just laughed and told her, "A better person than you I will be, and thank god I don't have to see you again." I smiled and walked away. Just like that high school years were over and I was ready to start fresh.

Right after graduation Jess, Maria, and I started to look for apartments to move in. All three decided to go to the same college. I was super excited to be moving out, even when my parents weren't happy about it. Everyone would tell me my parents' reaction was normal because they were worried about me, but it was more than that. They knew once I moved out they wouldn't be able to control me in what I do and don't. As well as make decisions for myself. All I wanted was more independence and for them to let me live my life without constantly reminding me I couldn't do certain things because of my disability. For example, date, go to parties, live in another city, and just explore life. We found an apartment in Fresno California and it was official I was moving out. I was so excited to be living on my own with my two high school friends. All three of us agreed to split the bills equally. I was a little nervous for the fact that my parents kept reminding I would always need help to do certain things. My mind kept thinking, "If I ask for help to change and they look at me *eww*. What if they get tired of me?

Moving day was here and I was so excited. We moved on July 1st because we would be starting school on July 5th. The apartment was a one-bedroom apartment and all three beds fit perfectly. Our parents helped us move in but we were ready for them to leave so we could officially start this new chapter of our lives. The first few days were going great and we were getting ready to go to our first day of class. I got to my first class of the day which was math class and that's when I quickly started realising I might have picked the wrong school. When I walked into the classroom all I saw was a room filled with computers. So I figured we would have to do our class work on the computer and it wasn't a big deal. I sat down and I thought the professor would give us a lecture on what we would be learning, but that didn't happen. Instead, the professor just introduced herself and told us to get to work. I was so confused I was like, "You are not going to teach us? How are we going to learn the material?" This made me nervous because I wanted to pass the class but if she was not teaching us is going to be more difficult. This is when another red flag appeared that I might have picked the wrong school. Math class lasted three hours and those three hours were the longest three hours ever. I walked out of that class so confused, disappointed, and sad because I wanted to learn and I felt that I didn't learn absolutely anything. I had an hour's break between my next class. I stayed on campus. I went to the cafeteria to kill time and everyone would just stare at me. I felt so uncomfortable and wanted to go home. I was nervous my English class was going to be like my math class. I walked into my English class and saw computers and I was like, "Oh great here we go again." I was already disappointed and I didn't want to stay there. The professor started the class and I was just waiting for him to tell us we can get to work, but he didn't. I got excited because the professor had a lecture plan and was teaching the class. I told myself "See it gets better this is what my college class should be." My English class was over and I could go home. My first day of college was over and even when it started not so good I was content to be here. I was starving I hadn't eaten anything since the morning and couldn't wait to go home and eat.

A few weeks passed and living with two roommates wasn't going how I expected it to be. I would be at school for hours and when I would come home all I wanted to do was eat. Unfortunately, most of the time when I got home the food for that day was gone. They would eat without me or eat my part. The first few times it happened I was like, "Okay maybe they didn't cook enough." It kept happening more often and I confronted them about it: "Hey why isn't food left for me? I brought my part of the groceries for the month and the food is almost gone and I have eaten most of the time."

They told me, "Oh we thought since you spend most of the day in school you eat over there." "Yes I have snacks over there, but I wait to come home and eat dinner," I told them. The food situation kept happening and it was bothering me.

At this time I was officially dating Issac he didn't go back to Puerto Rico after we graduated high school. I was happy he also moved to Fresno close to my apartment. So when the food situation didn't change with my roommates I would just go to Issac's place every day after school. Since I wasn't consuming the groceries I was paying for I stopped buying groceries. I just brought snacks and some meals I could do in the microwave. My roommates started to get upset that I started to only buy snacks and frozen meals. They told me, "Paola, why aren't putting your part of the groceries? That's not the deal we had." I responded, "Yes, you are right it wasn't part of the deal and you guys keep eating all the food without leaving some for me that wasn't part of the deal either." Both of them didn't say anything just stayed quiet. I told them, "Since I don't eat here I won't be providing the same amount of money for groceries, I think that's fair."

"Oh and don't worry I won't touch your guy's food."

They told me, "Omg why are you being like that?"

"I'm not being mean I just think is better like this."

A few days had passed since I had that conversation and I started to notice them acting weird towards me. Every time I would walk in the living room or kitchen they would stop talking. I quickly figured they would be talking about me. I started to feel depressed and unhappy where I was living.

Also, the first semester was over and I passed all my classes. The thing was I was unhappy at school too. I realised it wasn't what I expected and wanted. I started my second semester, but I wasn't paying attention in any of my classes. Quickly into my second semester, I was already failing my computer and math classes. I was spending a lot of time with

Issac and avoiding going to my apartment the most I could. Since I hardly ate proper meals I started to lose weight and I looked sick. During this time I also avoided going to my parents' house because I didn't want them to notice what was going on. The reason was they were going to tell me, "Te dijimos que esto iba a pasar" (We told you this was going to happen), and honestly I didn't want to hear it. I kept pretending everything was good, but inside I was dying. I started to blame my disability for my roommates treating me like they were. The anger that I thought I left behind of myself during my early high school years was back and stronger. Due to us sharing a room, I would wait until they would go to sleep to step out to the living room and cry until I fell asleep on the couch. This quickly became my nighttime routine. I was falling into a depression. I would find any excuse to miss class and stay home when my roommates were in school, so could I cry alone. My relationship with Issac was also falling apart. I kept avoiding him and he started to go out a lot more to places I wasn't okay with. One day in English class the professor started to explain the importance it was to be doing your research on the college you decide to go to because it can determine how valuable your degree will be if you obtained your degree from a creative school. He also explained how our school wasn't that creative and that applying for a master's or another bachelor's at a different school was going to be so hard. A super red flag appeared in front of me and I was like "I have to leave this school now."

The next day I went to talk to my counsellor about what I heard and the major I signed up for because I didn't like it. I was in shock by what she told me "Paola if you transfer to another college the credits you have done won't transfer."?

The blood left my body because not only did I waste my money, time, and mental health. I was doing a major I hated and the major I wanted they didn't offer. Plus, the credits I did here won't count elsewhere it would be like starting from the bottom.

I quickly made an appointment at the community college back where my parents lived. I applied and I could start the following semester. I didn't even bother to finish my current semester all I wanted was to get out of there. Even when it meant moving back to living with my parents. I told my roommates I was moving and of course, I was going to pay my end of the rent and bills before I left. They took it good or so I thought. I told Issac I was moving back home and we weren't going to see each other as often. His response was, "Why does it matter if we still don't see each other." I didn't like the tone he said it very angrily. He then proceeded to tell me, "I'm leaving back to Puerto Rico with my parents, tu no me quieres aquí." I have no idea where he got the idea that I didn't want him here. I was hurt for him thinking that and sad he was going away so far. I asked him "So you still want to be together or are we breaking up?" Deep down all I wanted to hear "We are still together," but he said, "I don't know. Let's just take it day by day." I moved out so confused and hurt.

9

I had a few weeks I had move back to my parent's house. I wasn't going to school because I had to wait until the new semester started. Meanwhile, I had to finish registering for classes at Merced Community College. I went to campus to turn in some papers for financial aid I ran into a friend from high school and to my surprise she told me what my old roommates were saying. "Paola, Jess told us how you left without telling them and you would never pay your full part of the bills." I was speechless and angry because that wasn't true at all. I all said, "Oh really, they do not tell you how they would leave me without food, eat all my groceries, and yet I'm the bad person." The rest of the day I had that on my head. The rumours they were spreading around. I mean I'm used to having rumours spread about it because Mitchell did that to me all the time in high school. This rumour was getting to me because I was nice to them regardless of how they treated me. Since I moved I didn't hear from them ever again. My depression was getting the best of me. I had so much time on my hands and hearing my family tell me "I told you so" every chance they had made me so angry with them and myself. I would look in the mirror and I didn't like myself. I was missing Issac so much and since he moved back to Puerto Rico I hardly heard from him. The thought that would always cross my mind was "Oh he probably found someone else," "a normal girl." The anger of me being "different" just would get the best of me. I would cry at night questioning "Why do I have to be like this? Why?" I would question this every single night. I also got good at masking what I was really going through. I would always smile for others and would get comments "omg you are always happy." Deep down I wasn't it.

The first day of my spring semester at Merced College was here. I was so nervous for many reasons. The main reason was "Is it going to be like my previous college?" Also not have a TA to help me take notes, but I solved that issue a day before. I hired a girl to just help me with the note-taking. I was still in shock the college didn't offer these services and I had to pay out of my pocket. I didn't have a job at the time so I was paying my note-taker with my financial aid money. Yes, the money I needed for books was going to my note-taker. I went to my first class and the stares didn't fail. I was looked at as the strangest thing they have ever seen. I didn't mind because it was a "normal" college class. What I mean by this is the professor was giving a lecture and we the students were taking notes.

I quickly got into a routine and it helped distract me from my other thoughts. Adjusting to the real college life was hard. I started getting comparisons from professors. I had to prove to them I was capable of learning the material just like everyone else in the class. I also started having problems with My TA she got the information I was receiving SSI. This money is from social security. She thought I was receiving a huge amount and I was rich. So she wanted more and I couldn't afford to pay her more. I couldn't because that SSI money was getting deposited to my parents and they decided how it got spent. Second, it wasn't a huge amount, it was enough to cover rent and food. I told her "I'm sorry I can't pay you more right now, maybe next semester." She didn't take it well because after this she started to make offensive comments here and there. One day during our break she told me "You are only able to come to college because of me, look at you everyone feels bad for you." I didn't respond. I was trying so hard to hold my tears back. I was so tired of getting put down by people. I went home and I cried the rest of the day in my room. I only had a week left of classes so I decided I wasn't going to put up with my TA. So I text her "Hey I won't need you to come with me to my classes anymore. Thank you for your help. You can pass by anytime to pick up your payment. I got no response. I followed by doing something I had never done before. I took the community bus in my electric wheelchair all by myself. On the way to campus, all I was thinking was how I was going to ask a classmate for notes if I needed them. I got to my only class of the day and we didn't do much because we were preparing for finals. I was proud of myself for not letting my fear get the best of me. Like "See you took the bus. You got to campus and home safe." This made me get a little confidence in myself. It felt so good. I did all my finals and I passed all of them. I told myself "¡Sí se pudo! You got through the first semester, it can't be worse than this."

Summer started and I thought it was going to be like

every summer home bored without seeing my friends. I was on Facebook just killing time when I received a message from Issac "Hey chica te quiero ver." I smile so quickly. He wants to see me. I quickly responded, "Yes, when?" He responded "Tomorrow." I told him "Yes see you tomorrow I can't wait to see you." I finally had something to look forward to. I hadn't seen him in over 6 months since he left back to Puerto Rico. We had so much to talk about. I knew he dated other girls, but we weren't together. I genuinely care for him as a friend he has always been a good friend to me. The next day came and went to Starbucks we agreed to meet up. I saw him and couldn't help but just smile. I did realise I didn't feel butterflies like I did at first. Issac always made me comfortable talking to him about anything. He said he moved back and is going to Merced College. I was so excited because I was going to have a friend on campus. "You look so pretty I miss seeing your face." He then kissed me. I was confused but happy. Maybe if we started dating again everything else would fit in. I will be more "normal." After this coffee date, Issac and I started talking every day. I didn't feel as alone, but I started noticing my feelings weren't the same. He also would make comments comparing me to the other girls he dated. "Is normal" I would tell myself. Did it bother me yes, but I didn't tell him.

The first day of my second semester was here and again I was nervous because I had to deal with all the stares again. This semester I was officially a full-time student. I wasn't prepared for what I was going to live. I got broken so much and put myself together. You will understand what I mean. I went to my first class Spanish. Issac was taking this class with me, which made me more comfortable having a familiar face. At this time we were taking a break he kept talking to other girls and honestly, I wasn't going to keep telling him to stop. When we entered the class I saw him and he saw me. We locked eyes and just had a feeling that went through my body.

10

———————

Ivan had a big part in how I would see relationships now. Our relationship was at first sight. He has the most beautiful green eyes and the most charming smile. I couldn't help but blush every time I saw him. After class, I went around campus to kill time and I ran into him. "Hi," he said I was screaming inside. He said hi and smiled and I said hi back. You might be asking why are you surprised he said hi. Well, earlier in class we had to introduce ourselves to the class. Once I opened my mouth everyone looked at me so weirdly. Due to my cerebral palsy, my speech was affected, so when I talk and I'm nervous I sound more weird. I mean I already stand out as a girl who moves weirdly and uses a wheelchair. Now you add my speech I feel like a walking sign that "says yes look at me I'm weird." My speech was another big insecurity of mine because it brought attention to me, but now it makes me stand out. So when Ivan said hi I was shocked. He proceeded to sit next to me and asked "Why are you alone?" "Oh, I'm just waiting for my next class." In reality, I had no friends to kill time with except for Issac but he was in class. Ivan then asked me "What's your next class?" and I told him Psychology. I showed him my schedule and he told me "I know where that building is let me walk you." What? He wants to walk me to my class. I was in shock and my dumb self couldn't stop smiling.

I was in shock still when he approached me. Had to put that aside and focus on this class. The professor hadn't even finished introducing the course when I knew this was my major. Introduction to psychology made my soul light up. The feeling was unexplainable all I knew it made me excited and happy. Like I found my purpose in life. I went home excited and happy this semester was going to be different. To my surprise, I got a message on Facebook and I checked it was Ivan. I quickly got up to see the message. Yes is him. I was smiling and nervous I didn't know if I should answer him. I'm not good at talking to guys. I opened the message and to my surprise, he was asking if I had done the homework. I was like "Ohh, but hey he looked me up on Facebook or it's just his excuse to start a conversation." This should been my first red flag. I passed him the homework and he only replied with a "See you in class." I smiled, but I was like "I don't get a thank you?" The next day in class he didn't even say hi. He was avoiding eye contact. In my mind, I was thinking "Did I do something? Or do I look ugly today?" I tried so hard to pretend the form he was acting wasn't bothering me. Once the class was over he ran out and I quickly thought "His trying to get away from you." I was so mad at myself for thinking he liked me. I realised my disability was going to get in the way of dating. "Another thing you going to take away from me." At 19 years yes I felt my cerebral palsy had taken so much from me and now this. My heart instantly broke. Another aspect of my life that wasn't going to be normal. During this semester I had to drop half my class due to not having a note taker and my fear of using my nose to take notes because I didn't want to get even more stares during class. I was sad and angry because I was getting behind on my degree. My mind went to "You not going to graduate." I was so frustrated with myself that I wasn't enjoying my life. I felt numb all I could think "What more is this disability going to take away from me?"

I was sitting in psychology class the professor was talking about low self-esteem, depression, and disabilities. She locked eyes with me while she said "People with disabilities belong in a society like we do. They are capable of providing for society. They are set aside in this world and we got so much to learn from them." This made me think about what I wanted to do with my degree and life. I knew I was capable of so much more and I needed to stop caring about standing out due to my disability, this could be a good thing. The semester was almost finished and I pulled through. I told myself if other people feel bad for you, you shouldn't so stop feeling bad for being born with a disability. Instead, embrace your disability. Cerebral palsy doesn't go away, so if with me for life let's start making the best of it.

11

———

Spring 2013 I made a big change that led me to start embracing my disability. I always find ways to adapt to either using something, or the environment and coming up with new ways to do things. I figured since I type with my nose why not take my iPad and just do it? You get stares regardless so why not take notes by yourself with your nose and stop worrying about finding a note-taker Yes I went to my spring semester mentally prepared for the extra stares I would be getting for doing this. I was determined to obtain all the credits I needed to transfer to a CSU to get my bachelor's. In all this, you might be asking if I had changed my mindset on dating. Well no I still think my disability is getting in the way of my dating life. Ivan and I have become a thing, but he asks me to keep it down on the low. I agree. I liked him so much and he knew how to charm his way.

I went to my first class and like usual I got stares like "Look that girl in the wheelchair." I sometimes wished I could tell them yes and what. I don't do it because I don't like being rude and bringing more attention to myself. The professor started talking and was having a difficult time taking out my iPad. My mind was going crazy. "Omg, Paola can you do something right." "See now everyone is looking at you."Even the professor was staring at me and all I did was smile. I wanted to run out of there. I pushed through it and I did manage to take out my iPad to take notes. At this point, I started taking notes and I honestly didn't care about the stares. The reason was that they were already staring and I was more focused on not missing important information. This class was over and I only had 10 minutes to get to my next class. All I did on my way was think of ways I could take my iPad faster without making so much noise. One thing about having cerebral palsy it made me super creative and think quickly on the spot to accommodate something to my needs. I did exactly that in my next class. I thought I only had to deal with my classmate's stares, but that wasn't the case. My math professor was uncomfortable with the way I was taking notes. I will never forget what he said next. "This class is not easy, if you are not capable of learning don't take someone else to spot." He was looking me in the eyes the entire time he was talking. That message was directed towards me. I was like "Okay bring it on" so not only I had to prove to my classmates I belonged there just as they did, but I had to prove to my professors as well. I thought I was over that obstacle, and that college was going to be different. Once again I felt I didn't fit in. I saw everyone walking with a friend and me ninety-five percent of the time I was alone. Ivan didn't want to hang out with me on campus. Issac had different classes and he started dating Ivan's sister. I become really good friends with them. At times it would hit me how alone I felt, but I was so focused on proving to others I was going to be successful in college, that I just bottled all my feelings down.

When I decide to not depend on having a note-taker and do it myself with the method that works for me. I also adventure in finding my transportation to get me from point A to B. Taking the community bus I met my best friend Jasmine. Jasmine and I agree that if I had been on the bus this semester we wouldn't have met. Our friendship was like we had known each other for years. Jasmine and became so close quickly. Many people assume that if someone is Friends with a person with disabilities is automatically due to pity. Wrong we can build true friendships and relationships just like everyone else. Jasmine would get as if she wouldn't get embarrassed to go out in public with me. This question didn't bother me it just made me laugh at how ignorant people are still in the 21st century. Jasmine and I shared so many similar experiences and I felt she truly understood me. Meeting her has to be one of the best things that could have happened from me attending Merced College.

Also, from my friendship with Jasmine, I began to realise I was surrounded by people who called themselves my "friends", but in reality, they only used me for their convenience. I was the friend who was looking for me to help them with homework or get their work done. When it came to me needing their help my so-called "friends" would disappear. There were many occasions I was left out of things because they felt embarrassed to hang out with me. From that moment on I kept my circle of friends small. I have people in my corner who believe in and support me in my goals. The stereotype that our lives are lonely and boring isn't true because we are more than our disabilities. On many occasions, I'm the one with the crazy plans and up to breaking the rules. My close Friends found it funny how their parents wouldn't question them where we were going because to their parents I was so innocent and calm I wouldn't dare to break rules, but only if they knew I was the plan master of all our wild adventures.

Therefore, I would tell Ivan how I felt and he would tell me to stop being dramatic. Then tells me how he loves me. He knew how to pull me in because he knew I didn't complain about his behaviour. All this started affecting my grades in some of my classes, but I didn't give up. I felt every semester I had so many obstacles to overcome I kept asking, "What more is there on my way to not getting to my goal?" I would cry at night just wondering why there were so many obstacles. I question if this was a sign that achieving a higher education was not for me. I had no one to talk to. I didn't feel comfortable talking to Ivan either. Our relationship was becoming toxic. There was verbal and psychological abuse. He would complain about the way I kiss him "Eww you can't even do that right." I would text him during class and he would respond with "Leave me alone, stop being annoying." I tried doing what other girls did to see if it would make him happy, but for him it was ridiculous. I got pushed down at school, personal life, at at home. I couldn't catch a break. My parents didn't make it easier for them I'm only good for school and that's all I should be doing. I understood the sacrifice they made for me to be able to a an opportunity to achieve a higher education. I will always be grateful because if we had stayed in Mexico I wouldn't have been able to do the things I have accomplished. At this age, during this time I felt they weren't letting me live my life. Explore the world because they would tell me "Nunca sabes lo que te puede pasar. I hated they used the excuse that you never know what can happen, especially if you have a disability. Due to this, I started hiding more stuff from them and lying about places I was going. I did this because I was 21 years old and if I wanted to go to a party my friends had to come ask them for permission. This was so embarrassing. At this time I was legal to consume alcohol and fun I "fitted" when drinking alcohol. The group of friends I hung out with thought it was cool that I could drink. This led me to drink from Thursday to Sunday because that is what "college life" was. I also was drinking to forget how Ivan treated me. I was using alcohol to help numb me from my feelings. One day we were good another he was cheating on me. Yet I stayed because he would tell me "You know I'm the only one that's going to want you like that. You won't find anyone else that puts up with your weird disability." I believed him for almost four years I stayed in this abusive relationship because I was afraid I wouldn't find love again. This wasn't love, it was more of me trying to hang on to the idea I had to have a boyfriend to be more normal and fit in. Leaving Ivan hurt so much because I pictured my life with him and I grew an attachment to him, but I knew this wasn't love and I deserved better. We both wanted different things and I was so close to transferring to a CSU that I knew deep down things between us would have gotten worse.

12

———————

erced College kept adding classes to my academic requirements to transfer. At times I felt they were doing it on purpose because I made friends in my major and they didn't have to take some of the classes I was told I needed to take. I was so frustrated because I had been in this college for almost five years and all I wanted was to get out. On the bright side by this time I was comfortable taking notes on my iPad using my nose. All my work was also done with my nose. This method had worked so well for me, that it was getting me through college. I thought that was cool. I was finally in my last semester at Merced College and I couldn't be more excited. I can see the light at the end of the tunnel. Everything was going smoothly this semester. I applied to CSU Stanislaus for a bachelor's in psychology. My application was accepted. For once in a long time I finally felt everything was falling into place. I had so many obstacles just to get here and I was so glad I didn't give up. Many times I was about to. I even stopped believing in myself, but that urge I had to prove wrong to those who told me wasn't going to do it was keeping me going. In May 2016, I walked crossed the Merced College stage. I officially obtain my Associate's degree. I kept telling myself "You did it."

I was proud of myself I didn't give up despite all the obstacles I had to face. I agree college is not easy for anyone, but I had to work twice as hard to prove I deserve to be there. I could only imagine how is going to be at CSU Stan. Summer 2016 was just preparing for the transition. I attended the new student orientation and right from the start, I got a different vibe. I liked the feeling and right away I made friends. During this time I was more focused on my education than dating. I still was heartbroken from my last relationship. Seeing him at CSU Stan made it difficult to get over my feelings, but I also knew I didn't want to be with someone that treated me the way he did. I was starting to stand up for myself a little more. The last night of summer before I went back to school my friend had a BBQ and she insisted she had someone she wanted me to meet. I already had a suspicion it had to do with a guy. I was not interested in being the entertainment of another guy again. For guys, I was a toy to play with. I had real feelings like everyone else. Due to my disability, I was seen as an easy target, but realise I played a part in that. By this I mean I wanted to fit in so badly and feel "normal" that I let a lot of things pass by because hey at least he was talking to me. My mindset was changing. So went I went to this BBQ the guy she wanted to meet mostly took one look at me and ignored me. I was okay with that. Mari saw me and told me "Look this Ariel, his Robert cousin." "Nice to meet you," I told him. He hugged me and "Nice to meet you, que bonita eres." I low-key blush. He told me I was pretty and he stayed there actually making conversation with me while everyone was looking. I found out he lived 5 hours away in Los Angeles. My heart sank a little. This meant I probably won't see him again. I don't know why I feel like this. "Paola calm down his much older than you, a guy like that would never be interested in you." Thinking of my history with all the guys I had something to do I always ended up getting played and I was tired. I had a nice time at the BBQ and before I left Ariel asked me for my number. Yes, I gave him my number but I doubted he would text me.

I got home that night and I had a text from Ariel. I wonder what he wanted if I text back. He replies "I know your birthday is this week. I will be in town can I take you out?" "How do you know is my birthday? I was turning 24 and still was processing that he was 30 and talking to me. I knew Marie told me about my birthday because we had plans to go out. On my birthday it was the only date I didn't have to ask my parents for permission to go out. Yes, I still had to ask them and most of the time they said no, so I hardly went out. I miss out on a lot of things people my age are doing because of them. I was scared to stand up to my dad because would always be yelled at and he would still spank me from time to time. I stop asking. I would stay home or if I was going out I would lie where I was going. So I told Ariel I had already plans and he was welcome to enjoy. He said yes. I was excited about my 24th birthday. Ariel sounded mature and knew what he wanted in life which attracted me to him. I was excited to possibly be starting a new relationship, but I couldn't lose focus on my school. I was barely starting my first semester at CSU Stan and I had to adapt to this new environment. I adapt quickly and I felt comfortable here. Classes were kicking my ass, but the professor gave me the same treatment and that's what I had been wanting. Ariel and I have been talking more and more. He would make comments like "We going to have an amazing future together." "You are what I have been waiting for." I would blush and I felt happy. Finally, I'm happy with someone. Ariel would come to visit town once a month. He wouldn't come to my house. I would meet him at Marie's house or the mall. I was getting tired of meeting somewhere else and I thought it was time for him to meet my parents. I told him and I didn't expect him os say "I rather not, let's take it slow a bit longer." I was confused and I didn't want to be a pushy girlfriend. So I decided to just go along with it.

On the other hand, I always struggled to ask for help in public because I didn't want to be a bother to others. On campus, there was a Starbucks and I wanted to buy a coffee one day. My dilemma here was how I was going to give her my card to pay and how I was going to grab my order if I couldn't grab the cup with my hands. Maybe a few months earlier I wouldn't consider going to buy something by myself just because I didn't want to be an inconvenience to others. I was sitting in the library and thought to myself "Paola you want that coffee go get it, stop limiting yourself just because you do things differently." I got my wallet, took my card and I put it between my fingers. I knew I could hold it like this and I would just hand it to the cashier. I was nervous on my way to Starbucks. "What if they don't want to take my order? "Hopefully is not packed." I get there and is packed. My turn was next to order and I ordered my coffee. I extended my hand to the cashier and I handed her my card. She right away got it and to my surprise, she put it back between my fingers just as I had it. I was so surprised. I thanked her and waited for my order. The hard part was how was I going to grab my cup to put it on my cup holder in my wheelchair. I couldn't grab it with my mouth it was too heavy. So I decided I was going to ask the cashier if she could put it on my cup holder. Yes, this was hard because I didn't like to bother others, but I told myself it was okay to ask. What's the least they can tell me? No. My order was ready and I asked "Sorry can you put it in my cup holder? Please, is hard for me to grab it. "Yes, of course." "Thank you so much." I rolled in my wheelchair so happy. "See Paola you did it." I realise asking for help when you need it is not a bad thing. This event made buying my coffee by myself it gave me so much confidence in myself. I started to embrace my disability. Yes, it might have taken me a good while, but at 24 years old I realised my cerebral palsy makes me unique and that wasn't a bad thing at all. Now every morning I would go buy myself a coffee before class. I also started eating in the cafeteria by myself. The way I feed myself is unique. I picked the food with my mouth. I was aware some people looked at me, but I stopped caring. All I would say in my mind was "Yes I do things differently and what?" My mindset changed and I felt comfortable in my skin. I stopped seeing my disability as burned.

13

———

A year passed and I was about to start my last year of undergrad at CSU Stan. The school was going well. I loved my psychology classes and I started picturing myself as a therapist in the future. You might be asking how your dating life is. My relationship with Ariel became on and off. He started making excuses as to why he couldn't come visit. Since my family would go to Los Angeles to visit family I would take that chance to see him. At times it seemed like it would bother him that I would show up at his place without telling him. I would do it as a surprise. I told myself "Maybe he doesn't like surprises." Then I started thinking he was cheating on me. I confronted him about it multiple times he denied it. He would tell me "Está loca." To him, I was being crazy and it was a constant argument. I would constantly question "Why I'm not enough?" "Why do I always have to be the problem especially when I express my feelings? I felt my point of view wasn't important. Maybe if we finally have sex like he wants things would change. The reason I hadn't had sex was many reasons. The main ones were most of the time he wanted to have sex with me he was drunk and if I was going to lose my V-card I wanted him to be sober. Second, when he wasn't drunk he would pressure me and I didn't feel comfortable. There were times he would touch my parts like forcing himself and I just didn't like that. He would tell me how when I graduated we were going to move in together and how lucky he was. When we were away he would be so sweet and due to his job, he traveled a lot. I wanted him to come to my house but he would make all the excuses. When he would come was only at night. Then he started to only want to go in public at night. I started to grow suspicious about it. I confronted him about it and he told me "is your fault we get dirty looks." This is when the relationship was getting toxic. He was embarrassed to be seen with me in public during the day. His reasoning was during the day more people could see us. His words hurt me because I truly thought finally I found someone who didn't care about my disability he met me like this and out of nowhere now it was a problem for him, but I guess he was just that good at hiding it. The relationship just kept getting worse. He would come to visit his family in town and wouldn't tell me. So he wouldn't come to visit me. I never asked him for anything, but I was a big fan of Maluma and he was going to have a concern in Los Angeles. I begged him that we should go. He would say "No I work late. There's going to be a lot of people." I was really upset and angry he never wanted to go anywhere anymore. My suspicion of him cheating kept growing. I got tired of putting up with the way he was treating me instead of keeping quiet like I did in the passed. I talked to him and told him I didn't like the way he was treated and that I didn't lie to him about my disability. He met me like this I didn't understand why he had a problem now. He apologised and assured me he loved me and things were going to change. A few days later he surprised me with tickets to the concert. I was so happy and this was a sign that things were going to change. The night of the concert was epic. We had so much fun and he was being so sweet with me. I had hope for us. That night he promised he was going to make it to graduation. He knew how important that day was for me. This didn't last long he didn't come to graduation. No call or text to at least congratulate me. A week later he called he told me he had a work trip that he couldn't get out of. I didn't believe him anymore I was tired of his behaviour with me I decided to confront him one last time. A few weeks I went to Los Angeles to visit family. I lied to my parents I was going with a friend, but I was going to his apartment to surprise him. I had a key. I was the one surprised. He had another girl in there. I walked in on them having sex, but it wasn't any girl. It was my biggest high school bully, Mitchell. My heart sank. They both just laugh at me. Mitchell said "I give him what you can't. He is disgusted by you.? I didn't know what to do I just left crying. I was so humiliated, angry, and broken. I questioned, "Why me?" "Why again?" "Why do I always end up getting played?" I was so hurt and I lost hope in love.

14

───────

Spring semester 2018 was almost coming to an end. This semester had been one the toughest for me academically. I was taking 21 units. Yes, I was crazy, but I didn't want to walk on graduation and come back next semester for one class. I still couldn't believe I was graduating despite all the obstacles that kept showing on my path. One was transportation, especially during the rainy season. My university was a 25-minute drive, but since I don't drive I had to take two community buses. The normal 25-minute drive would turn into a 2-hour commute on the bus. I also had to struggle with going to the bathroom on campus. Yes, the bathroom is something I was so insecure about because it was something I hadn't mastered doing without help. I would be off for the day on campus I obviously couldn't hold it until I got home. I realise I was able to pull down my pants if it was elastic band waist and only using my left hand. My left hand was the hand I had a little more control and semi-grab things. I still struggled with it and one of my biggest fears was to pee on my pants on campus because I couldn't pull my pants. Had to prove to some professors I deserve to be there and capable of passing the classes. Obstacles behind obstacles made me strong and it just motivated me more to get to the finish line. Everything I saw on the internet others were doing when they graduated it was my turn to do it. I waited almost 6 years since I started my college journey to have my graduation photo session. I wasn't going to let anyone ruin this for me, not even my breakup with Ariel. At CSU Stan I become more independent, my confidence boosted, and I learn to embrace my disability. CSU Stan not only educated me, but it gave me something more important self-empowerment. I would never forget some special words one of my professors told me "You are going to do epic shit in life."

On May 26, 2018, I became a first-generation graduate. I walked crossed that stage so proud of myself and I hope someday more individuals like me can do it too. One thing I always wanted was to make my parents proud and show them I can do much more. Also with me graduating, I thought they would give me more freedom to live my life as a grown adult, but I quickly found out it wasn't happening.

15

Now that I officially graduated with my bachelor's degree the adulting life was about to start. I underestimated how hard it was going to be to find a job. I didn't waste any time. I began to apply for jobs in my area. All jobs I took a look at would ask for experience and I didn't have any. I was fresh out of college. I started to worry and think "What if I don't find a job?" I also had my parents pressuring me to now work on what I obtain in my major. I quickly realised with a BA in psychology I was limited because I didn't have my license, which most employers places were asking. "Do I want more school?" Another thing I encountered while seeking employment was discrimination. Yes, discrimination because I have a disability. "Here I go again having to prove I deserve the position and capable of getting my work done." I was about to be 25 years old and I was so exhausted constantly having to prove myself to others that I'm more than what they see as my disability. Until this moment I thought my disability wouldn't be such a big deal to find employment because we are all adults and a disability doesn't define someone's abilities and skills. There is a reason why the state of California established the ADA Act. When researching for employment I learned about the Americans with Disabilities Act and it was the most ironic thing. You asked me "Why is it ironic Paola?" this act is specifically established to prohibit discrimination against people with disabilities in several areas including employment. When I finally got an interview for an agency I have been wanting to work at. I showed up to the interview and literally when I walked into the room the people that were there stared me down from head to toe. In my mind, I was "Yes I have a disability, but I'm going to show you what I can bring to the table." I didn't let their staring intimidate me. I answered all their question. I didn't get stuck on any of them. I walked out of there feeling good about how I did on my interview. A few days passed and I finally got a response back I didn't get the position. When I read the reasoning of why I laughed of anger. "You meet all our qualifications. You would be a great addition everywhere, but we are looking for someone who makes our clients comfortable." All that came out of my mouth was "WTF" I was so confused. The entire message was covering the truth. The reason I didn't get the position was my disability and it was so clear to me. I was sad, confused, angry how can still in 2018 I have to be battling this? The entire situation was going against the ADA Act which is meant to protect me, but I realised employers don't care about laws not protecting our rights because to them we aren't important to society. This only gave me the motivation to keep pushing and knocking on doors.

I came across an ad for a part-time advocate position for foster children. I read over the job duties and it sounded like something I could do. I didn't see myself working with foster children, but it could be a chance to get my feet wet on gain work experience. I showed up to the interview ready to kick ass. The interview went great. I was honest when they asked why my interest in working around the foster care system. They asked me to wait. I thought they were going to call me, but I guess they were deciding right in there. I got the position and they explained the position was more like an internship. Honestly, I was all for it. I looked at it as a great opportunity to gain experience, learn new things, and be able to help others I can do this. Building my career was my motivation and I had to start somewhere. Of course, the salary wasn't what I wanted, but it was an internship and I knew this was just to start with.

In September 2018 I started working at CASA as a court-appointed advocate. The training was intense and very interesting. There was a lot of responsibility and I was ready to take on this responsibility. I finished my training and was sworn in as a court advocate. This meant I could officially start getting assigned cases. The first month I spent working at CASA gave me more confidence and it gave me an outlet to forget about my problems. I was still heartbroken and it didn't help running into him with her in town. I start to wonder if love isn't for me. I decided to focus on building my career and to stay single. I didn't want to date and open my heart to someone just to end up getting hurt again. I did exactly that.

After 2 months working with foster children, it pushed me to apply for my master's in Social Work. I had planned maybe to apply for my therapist license. However, working here inspired me to pursue social work. This career pathway would give me more freedom to choose the population I want to work with and is a career I can make a positive impact. I did the entire grad school application and waited 3 months to see if I got in. This graduate program only took 45 students per year. I was nervous because what if I didn't get in? I will have to wait for an entire school to re-apply. "Am I that smart to get into grad school?" I would think to myself. Three months passed on April 2019 I received an email and my heart sank when I read the first sentence. Unfortunately, I didn't get a spot and I was sad. I realised how badly I wanted this. I was doing this for me because I wanted to become the best social worker I could become. I analysed what I could do differently so I could be more prepared for the next round of applications. I was proud of myself for not letting this no get me down. Instead, it gave me more motivation to go for it because I knew I was capable of getting into that master's program. I went to the information meeting where they helped you with your application. The best decision I could have made because I learned the program didn't look so much at your grades, but more at your experience in the field and your statement. I only had 3 months of experience when I applied and I didn't include a letter of recommendation from my boss. I realised that was the mistake I made.

So I kept preparing for the new rounds of applications and learning all I could at work. The obstacle of not driving didn't stop me from doing my job. One of my job duties was to go to court when my client's case was being presented to the judge. Court started at 8;30 am and to get there on time I would take the earliest bus at six in the morning. This meant I would get up at four in the morning to get ready. I would do this for four days out of the week. When I had to do home visits I would take up to three buses just to get to my client's homes. I never missed any of my home visit appointments because I didn't drive. I took my job seriously because my clients had already been through so much trauma, that they needed their advocate to stay consistent. I would listen to their needs and advocate for them during their court dates. This job, brought me so much feeling of fulfilment on a professional level and a feeling of joy because I was making a positive impact on these kids' lives. Working at CASA gave me purpose and it opened my eyes that my calling was to help others and to be part of helping change the system. Also, it helped me realise as much as I have learned working here, I didn't see myself working as a social worker in the foster care system in the long run. This job is not for everyone. This job was emotionally draining because I was exposed to so many horrible situations my clients had to go through. Leaving your feelings at work was hard. This job required so much confidentiality because you are dealing with minors and legal stuff. After a year of working here, I re-applied for grad school and I already had in mind where I would like to work. I kept it a secret that I was re-applying because the first time I told someone I wanted to go to grad school they laughed at me and I got "Estás loca" "You can't go to grad school you're not that smart." All I did with this reaction was laugh and say "Watched me."

16

———————

The year 2020 was the year of so many unexpected things and events I was not expecting at all. I have been interested in content creation for a couple of years, but I have been hesitant to post videos because of my disability. In January 2020 I decided to create a TikTok account because I had friends who were constantly sending me videos and I couldn't see them. "Okay let's see what's all the hype about." I right away found this app interesting. Found that there were all types of videos makeup, fashion, comedy, lifestyle, etc. I came across a funny video and I could relate. So I tried to recreate it. "Why not post it? Who's going to see it you don't have any followers." I posted the video. I got a good laugh and it was a good distraction. I honestly didn't think the videos were going to get views, but to my surprise they did. I checked a week later I had 500 followers. Like what? I did that video just joking around because I was bored. So I started to post more videos here and there for fun. I gained more followers I was in shock that people were watching my videos. Then shortly after a worldwide event changed everything Covid-19 happened. A pandemic that was affecting everyone and taking so many lives. My job was affected by Covid. We completely started working from home. My clients were affected because we couldn't get that face-to-face interaction and they felt neglected. So, TikTok became my outlet to distract myself. I would post mainly comedy and fashion. All the videos didn't have my voice because I was so insecure about it.

In April 2020 two events happened in my life. I was waiting to hear back from grad school. I finally did. I received an email and I saw the notification I was so nervous to open it. I was alone in my room and I opened the email. "Dear Paola Garcia congratulations we are pleased to offer you..." I stopped ready and I started crying. I GOT IN. I GOT IN I kept repeating. I ran to tell my parents and the reaction I got from them I wasn't expecting. "Mamá, me aceptaron en la escuela." I had tears in my eyes "Ah, me asustaste! Yo pensé que era otra cosa." I was waiting for congrats, but no. I was so confused and mad. My mom came to my room later that night to congratulate me and how proud she was of me. I was so happy and I accepted the offer the next day.

A few days passed and I kept a secret from my friends but I finally told them. They were so happy for me and told me how proud they were. Marie did pull me aside and told me "I'm so proud of you. I always knew you were going to do big things. You deserve so much to be happy have you given a thought to getting back to the dating life?" I have been single for almost three years and I was scared to get hurt again. I told her, "Nah I'm good like this." "Paola, give yourself an opportunity, you deserve it." I honestly had pushed the idea of dating again because I was tired of getting used to and playing. Besides how was I going to meet someone if I hardly go out? I still had to ask my parents for permission and I got tired of fighting this battle with them. There was a global pandemic going on where we couldn't go out how was I going to meet someone? Yes. There were times I wish had someone in my life I was getting lonely. I wish had a significant other. To share important events like this. Simply share life with. I saw this far from happening.

The pandemic was getting worse and the only distraction was TikTok. On April 19, 2020, I decided to check my messages on TikTok, and most messages I got were creepy. The one that caught my eye was from a guy named Cristian. I checked his profile first, and from the picture I was "Like there's no way this handsome hot guy is messaging me." The reason his message caught my attention was because it wasn't creepy or dirty. The message was "Hi how are you?" I was intrigued and I answered him. I was surprised he answered almost immediately. I was in shock so I replied. His response was a clever way to find out if I was single. I smiled "Sorry for being weird you are so beautiful I had to text you lol with all the respect if you have a boyfriend." The conversation kept going for hours and I was enjoying it. He right away gave me his number and I don't know why, but I felt comfortable giving him the number. I don't why he gave me the feeling I knew him for a long time. Right away we started joking. He got my jokes and sarcastic. Even though I enjoyed our conversation I told myself "he is probably just bored and besides he lives in Florida I'm not doing long distance again." The next morning I woke to a text from him and it just made me smile so hard. We were having good conversations. Texting each other most of the day and I looked forward to his texts. "What's happening to you? You are becoming interested in someone you don't even know"

Talking to Cristian felt like a fresh breath of air. We had two weeks of texting and he still hadn't asked me what was wrong with me. He has seen videos and you can tell I have something different by the way I move. I question myself "Is it because he wants to play with me or because he doesn't care." I decided to ask him "It doesn't bother you if would be seen in public with me?" His response was "Why would I?" I told him because of my disability. His response "I don't see your disability to be you like everyone and besides I would be lucky to be out in public we the most beautiful woman." I was speechless. This is too good to be true a few weeks of texting he asked if he could FaceTime me and I panicked. I was so insecure about him to hear my voice which sounded weird. "What if he is like eww." So I lied I told him I was busy with work maybe another day. I felt bad. I wasn't looking for anything honestly our relationship naturally flowed between us.

The more we texted the more I liked him. I knew he was so far, but he was in the military and mentioned he was getting deployed to California in the summer. I didn't want to get hope, but I did want to meet him. Texting with Cristian has been so good, but I had to focus on starting grad school and I had a hard decision to make as well. I was nervous now because grad school is at another level I questioned myself if was going to be able to handle it. Also how school was going to be with COVID-19 because I wasn't a fan of virtual learning because in the past I did poorly in online courses. Virtual learning is not for me so starting grad school like that me nervous. Mostly I was proud of myself because I hadn't seen individuals like me attend grad school, so it was my opportunity to break that barrier and inspire others that they can also obtain their higher education. I started to think about where I wanted to do my internships and there was a place where I saw myself working and it means a lot to me. Central Valley Regional Center is a place I have been a client since I was little. This place offers services to individuals with disabilities and promotes independence for these individuals. I felt I could do great work here and it just got me excited to become a social worker. Since I have always had bad experiences with the different social workers I had. I wanted to gain all the proper training and tools to become the best social worker I could be.

17

———————

My love life until this point has been a disaster and I have been used for others' entertainment. So as I was realising my feelings for Cristian were getting stronger I was scared because I didn't want to get hurt again and I was discovering what real love felt like I didn't want to lose that. The connection I had with him is unexplainable I didn't have to hide or fake who I am and how I was. I was me and I was finally feeling like a part of my life was complete. Two months of texting, phone calls, and long FaceTime calls went by those months have been one of the best months in a very long time. We both were looking for something serious, but I wasn't pushing anything if it happens it happens. He has a daughter did made me a little nervous because obviously the baby's mother is involved and honestly I wasn't sure how that was going to go. I was one hundred percent open to having a friendly civilised relationship with her because I wanted all three of us to get along for the good of his daughter. I knew how important his daughter is to him and if we were going to get serious I knew it was something I had to do.

On June 13, 2020, Cristian asked me officially to be his girlfriend I was so happy and I still couldn't believe such a handsome guy like him wanted to go out with me. For the first time I felt I was in an actual relationship the feelings were different. I was scared my disability was going to scare him off, but I was like "I come with a full package." He constantly reassured he didn't see my disability he loved me the way I was. Honestly, at times I didn't believe him because I wasn't used to a guy telling me things like this especially out of nowhere. So there were times I didn't know how to respond to his compliments. After being played so many times by guys it was hard for me to believe his compliments. Especially when he promised to come visit in July and he kept pushing the date. I honestly started to think "Here we go again, his not taking our relationship seriously. Is a joke." I was getting upset and was scared of getting played again. We talked it out he had some things to resolve about his daughter and then he will be in California. The feelings I had for him were so strong it was scaring me. I was in love with a guy I met online how crazy is that? Swear I was not going to do long distance relationship again due to I went through with Ariel. I could talk to Cristian about anything for example, about my future career or what wanted to do with social media. He always encourages me to go for it. He believed in me and would always tell me, "Flaca you going to do big things, and be famous one day you have so much on you." "I'm your number one fan" It was so crazy to me that he believed in me so much only knowing me for a few months.

Dating long distances is hard especially when we are in different states. There were times were I wished he could tell me "Hey baby get ready I will pick you up to go get lunch." Sadly we could do that and would make me upset at times. Cristian was the fresh hair I needed at this time. I was never expecting to feel in love so hard the way I love him. He is the love of my life and now I know what it feels like to be in love. Those long FaceTime calls every day made up for the distance. In those hours it felt like we were in the same room. Since day one I saw how hard-working a man he is and his ambitions to have a better future attracted me so much about him. He is such a caring guy even though he might look tough on the outside. He is my teddy bear.

We constantly would plan to meet up and something always happened. I began to think we were never going to see each other and the long distance kept getting hard on me. At times it would upset me because it seemed it didn't bother him the long distance as much as it did me. "Maybe he doesn't want to see me as much as I do" I began to have thoughts like this one more often. My family wasn't helping either with these thoughts because when I told them about him I got, "He is just playing with you," "De seguro tiene a otra," "Amor de lejos, amor de pendejos," "He probably wants something," etc. I knew they were not going to support this relationship but their comments hurt and made me more insecure about myself. My parents would tell me they would tell me these things because all they wanted was to protect me because of my disability I was a bigger target to be taken advantage of. I was so tired of this point for them using my disability as an excuse to treat me like they did. Let me take my decisions, if I screw up that's on me. I needed and wanted to have full control of my life. I wanted my parents to know and see Cristian made me happy, but unfortunately, they didn't understand our relationship.

18

———————

Since I started grad school and got into a relationship 2,888 miles away from each other it was so many things to adjust to. The virtual school was hard to get used to because being in front of a screen in spam for 3 hours at a time was difficult. Paying attention in a loud Hispanic household was hard because as much as asked them to keep it down they wouldn't. I have always been a more hands-on visual learner so I do better in a classroom setup, but I had to find new ways to keep focus in class while being in my room. As aspiring social workers Covid was a perfect example that we have to adjust and get creative fast to find solutions because that is something we have to be able to do in the field. On the other hand, trying to make a priority my relationship with Cristian, to find time for us, and not let my school consume all my time and the distance get in the way of that was tricky at first, but we both made it work.

The most ironic situation I faced was in the first semester of my grad program. Part of the requirements was for us to do two internships, and different placements each school year. When my classmates started talking during the first of class about their placement I thought "Oh maybe I'm next to get a call for where I'm going to be working." I honestly didn't think anything of it.

Two weeks went by and nothing. I was starting to get nervous because the date for us to start our internship was around the corner. I finally received a call to go to my internship interview and I was relieved. My interview was at a school and I was okay with it even when a school wasn't on my list of places to do my internship. In the situation with COVID maybe the places I wanted weren't taking any interns. While I was doing the interview I felt she was looking at me up and down. I felt a little uncomfortable, but I had to nail this interview. I didn't hear from them after two weeks and when I did I was in shock, "Hi Paola unfortunately we can't have you as an intern here because the kids and parents will feel uncomfortable having a person like you around their kid. You're really smart and you will find a better place."

I had no words all I did was throw my phone and start crying out of anger. Once again I find myself being discriminated against because of my physical disability. This is who I am, is part of me, and is not going to disappear. Society needs to accept the fact people like myself are capable of much more and deserve equal opportunities like everyone else. The ironic thing was I thought my school would have my back because hello I'm in a social work program where advocating was a big part of it. Unfortunately, my school did the opposite they turned this on me. They blame me for having a disability and I had to fix it. My mind was blagged by the ignorance coming from a social work program that I was attending to better assist me in becoming the best social worker. I started to question if I should stay in the program not because I felt incapable of doing the work, but because I wanted to keep learning from "professionals" who blamed me for my disability instead of advocating for me. I wasn't going to let this get in my way of obtaining my master's degree. I had already missed more than a month of internship hours and it was too late to find a placement I was told by the program administration. I honestly think it was a lie, but I wasn't going to give up. I decided to take the option they gave me to postpone my first year of internship to the following school year and just focus on my academic classes. This meant I had to add one more year of grad school. I was really upset because it was so unfair I had to prolong my graduation an entire year just because the school saw my disability as "difficult" to find me an internship placement. This situation put me into a depression because I was so tired of the constant battles I had to fight because I had a disability I had to prove to others I deserved to be there. I earn my place like everybody else. Most importantly, I constantly had to work twice as hard for my work to be noticed as being equal level as my classmates. I was emotionally and mentally exhausted from constantly being compared to my peers because they saw me as "normal" and I "wasn't". "I am normal" I would yell inside. I wasn't heard, so I kept my feelings inside and this began to affect my relationship with Cristian. I was still processing the discrimination I was experiencing from my grad program and I started to pull away. I didn't open up to him because I didn't want to bother him with this issue. Also because I was scared I was going to scare him away. Also, I was used to keeping my problems to myself because, in my past relationship, they didn't care what I had to say, so it was hard for me to talk about my feelings. Because of these actions, he was getting signals that I didn't want to talk to him, I was cold towards him and he felt he had to pull teeth to get me to open up. This was our first fight. I didn't realise he was feeling like this. Also, I was having a difficult time with the distance I wanted to physically hug and kiss my boyfriend, especially during this time. I crave time with him, physical touch, going on dates and just spending time with him not via phone.

Everything kept building up inside of me. My insecurities began to appear in my relationship. My trauma from the past relationships was affecting me now. I sometimes thought he was cheating on me or he was going to get tired of me due to my disability. The long distance was hard on both of us and months kept passing without being able to each other. December came along and it was about to be six months of dating and we couldn't wait no longer to see each other. So we started planning a trip for me to go see him.

19

I knew my parents weren't going to let me go to Orlando Florida to see my boyfriend, especially alone. Yes, I know what many are thinking that I'm crazy for thinking of flying to another state to see a guy I met online. I understand before I met Cristian I would hear stories of people doing this and would think "They are crazy, I would never do that." Now I'm here about to do that. My parents would do anything to prevent me from going if they found out where I was going. I hated it lying where I was going, but I had no other choice. My best friend helped me with this. I told them she asked me to join her on a trip to Miami and that she was going for work purposes need a model because she does makeup. I was surprised because they told me okay. We booked the trip and I was so excited and nervous because I had never traveled except to Mexico.

January 14, 2021, was the day. When I sent him the text "the plane just landed" I had so many mixed emotions but mostly an excitement I couldn't explain. Those 5 minutes I waited for him to park the car felt like hours and all of the sounds I heard his car pull up. I saw him get out of the car and I felt butterflies. I was the happiest girl in the world. When we hugged it was the best feeling. I felt so much love and peace it was an amazing moment that I wish time could be frozen. He had a teddy bear and a rose for me. I couldn't stop smelling. My heart felt full. I wanted to cry but of happiness. He helped me get in the car and we took off to where we were staying. We both waited so long for this moment that we kept staring at each other. I was nervous too because I do need help with certain things and I didn't want to bother him by asking him for help. "What if he gets annoyed or tired of me asking for help" These thoughts were constantly on my mind, but he met me like this and I wasn't about to hide who I was. We got to the hotel and our room was upstairs and there was no elevator. I had a hard time with stairs I can go up or down by myself. He didn't think twice picked me up and carried me up the stairs. I was totally surprised by this. Once we settled in the room it finally hit me I was there with him. I couldn't explain my happiness. The first night I couldn't sleep because I had so many emotions and so many thoughts in my mind. Also, I wasn't used to sleeping with someone else. Before anyone thinks nothing happened that night. He was respectful and we enjoyed each other company. The next morning I was alone because he had gone to work. I started to think of creative ways I could get ready by myself so I wouldn't have to ask him. He checked on me and how I was doing and I had, to be honest, I needed help to get in the shower. He immediately told me to wait for him because he didn't want me to split my head open. He also told me he would close his eyes if that made me more comfortable. I laughed because I wasn't worried about him to see me naked. After all, he had seen my body before. When dating long distance you have to get creative to maintain intimacy that spark. I was more nervous about that aspect of having to ask him for his help to do something as simple as getting in the shower. I thought to myself "He probably going to get turned off by this." I wasn't going to let my mind get the best out of me on this trip. Once again I was surprised by his action he helped me without me asking and he was so respectful. I felt love, but I was not used to being treated like this at all. I was decently taken by surprise when he saw me brushing my hair and I had already decided to leave it down because I couldn't put it up and I didn't want to bother him. He just looked at me "I don't know how to do hair so are going to tell me how you want." I was speechless and right at that moment my heart felt full and I fell even more in love with him. I honestly didn't know how to act with him treating me like this. I was so taken aback nobody had done this before especially kissed me in public. This man is even helping me with my hair like what? How did I get so lucky?

I already knew he was the one, but on this trip confirmed it. He saw me as a woman, his girlfriend, and not the girl with a disability that I had seen all my life. Society has a stereotype that individuals with a disability can't have a regular sexual life. In reality, we can. We have the same urges as normal humans. I would be lying to you if told you I didn't get turned on by him. I did. I was honest with him since we started dating that I was a virgin. Yes, I was 28 years old and was still a virgin. I'm not ashamed of it. I felt forced in my past relationship to have sex with them. I didn't have sex with them because I didn't feel ready, I felt forced, they only wanted sex, and I wanted to be with someone who fully made me feel wanted in all aspects. Cristian made me feel wanted in all aspects, I knew I was ready, and most importantly if I was going to lose my virginity it was going to be with the person I truly was in love with. The night before I came back it happened. It was such a special moment, but some parts weren't how expected it to be. He was so sweet he was more concerned about it hurting me than enjoying the moment. I could tell he was holding back. I knew the first time it hurts is normal, but with cerebral palsy when having sexual intercourse it takes longer for the muscles to relax. That night I completely became his and he was mine. Yes, I will admit I wish it lasted a little bit longer. The same night he asked him to move in with him. Neither of us wanted to go back long distances, but I couldn't just miss my flight. We talked so much that last night we agreed to do things right and save as much money as we could so we could move together that summer. He was also going to talk to my parents and I was going to see how can I transfer school. I stare at him all night. We both were soaking in this moment of being together because we had to wait a few months to see each other again. When my alarm went on I started crying because I didn't want to go home. I didn't want to leave him. This weekend had been the best weekend I have had in a very long time. I felt complete, loved, and simply happy. I knew it was going to be hard to say goodbye, but it was so much harder than I thought. I felt that I left a piece of me behind. I cried on the flight.

I was back in California starting my second semester of grad school with a lot of changes happening. I wasn't sure if I was going to be able to transfer to a grad program in Orlando and my parents were not okay with that idea either. At this time I stopped sharing a lot of things with them because they didn't agree with the decision I was making. A few months after seeing each other Cristian and I had one of the biggest arguments and I thought our relationship was over. In a lot of conversations, he would always bring up his ex and at first, I didn't think anything of it. So it kept happening and it started to bother me because I felt in a way he was comparing me to her and it hurt me. I would think "He probably misses being with a normal girl" I wouldn't tell him anything I would just stay quiet. Until one morning we were talking and he said "I miss not having the family I could have had with my daughter and baby momma. I wanted to have a complete family..."

That lingered on my mind all day and finally, at night, I decided to tell him how I felt about it. He got really upset by what I had to say, but I all wanted was for him to see how it made me feel when he said that. Maybe I expressed myself wrong, but he told me he was tired of insecurities and me getting jealous over little things, but later I realised I wasn't wrong for feeling this way. When you have been through trauma and lies is hard to rewire your brain, so when he would make comments like these it brought me back to when I was with Ivan and Ariel. I had been used, lied to, and played with I was scared it was going to happen again. I was scared to lose him, but I was so hurt he was acting this way not answering and ignoring me. So I gave up. I turn my phone off for the entire weekend. I remember I cried myself to sleep all weekend long. I question myself why me and what did I do wrong? The following week I turned my phone back on. I see he texted me that he wanted to talk. "Probably he wants to break up with you I thought to myself."

All this was affecting my performance at school. I couldn't concentrate during classes, slacking on my home-work and mostly mentally checked out. This fight with Cristian and the problems with my family was getting to me. I started noticing all this stress was affecting my body I started losing weight, but I thought it was normal.

Cristian and I worked on things. I was trying to work on expressing myself better and not bottling things up. The moving together was still on the plans, but instead of me moving over there he was moving to California. He wanted a change and this was better for us. I knew deep inside this was going to bring problems due to his baby momma. I wasn't wrong. Cristian thinks I didn't notice but he began to slowly start disappearing on the weekends and I wouldn't hear from him until Monday. This all started more often when he decided it was better for him to move to California. I agree all couples need their space and alone time. I wasn't asking for him to be texting me every 5 minutes but at least a good morning and good night text. I wasn't getting that. I was getting instead messages left on read or delivered for days. One thing that bothered me more was when I didn't answer him he would quickly get mad, yet I had to accept him leaving me on read for days. I understand he needs quality time with his daughter and I'm all for it because he's an amazing dad and I can tell that little girl is his world. Seeing him with her made me so excited for our future and our kids. I knew he was going to be an amazing dad because he already was one. I knew something more was going on because the FaceTime calls started to disappear. Then he started to disappear for days during the week and I would text him and I would be left on read. On my 29 birthday, my suspicions of something was going on were confirmed. I received a text from him super late telling me to delete all our pictures from social media and that if his baby momma texted me to not respond because she only wanted to tell me lies. I was so confused but I didn't want to make the problem even bigger. I didn't delete the pictures. I just private them. Cristian again disappeared and I started to get more suspicions. Cristian told me a few days later that his baby momma found out he was moving and was taking him to court for child support. I believed him until he disappeared for a week and he blocked my number. I knew he was hiding something. I began to dig because I had a feeling in my stomach that this wasn't just because of the move but more of him not wanting me to find something out. What do you do when you dig? You find things you weren't ready to see and that's what happened to me. The things I encounter hurt me so much. The worst part was when all this was happening I was about to start my internship at a human services agency, but unfortunately, I couldn't focus on that because my mind was on what Cristian was hiding from me but why? Out of nowhere not hearing from him he called me that he needed two weeks to do some thinking and what he wanted. He told me to think if I wanted to be with him and deal with baby momma stuff. My heart broke I knew this meant we were breaking up. I wasn't wrong he decided to call me when I was working after two weeks of "thinking" and his reasons for breaking up were hurtful I will never forget his words. "I love you so much, you are such a great woman, and don't want to hurt you. I don't want to lose my daughter and you deserve better so starting now we going to be friends. I need time to figure things out so baby momma stops bothering you just tell her we never dated..." I lost it with that. That hurt so much "We never dated" like that easily we were nothing. He broke my hurt into pieces. The pain I felt was unexplainable, but I had to keep it together because I was at work. My mind kept replaying those words and my chest hurt. That day I cried so much and something told me there was more to the story. Important details he was hiding.

I checked my messages on Instagram and I see she sent me a message. I clicked on her profile and my heart broke, even more, I saw a very recent post caption that read, "Baby I love you." I saw posts of them out and about on the dates he would disappear, so I started putting the dots together. My heart had never hurt the way it was hurting at this moment. I truly love this man with all my heart and he played me like this. I was so hurt and broken and I started questioning if our relationship was ever real. A month passed by and I received a message from his baby momma rubbing it on my face that she had him and that I was just a joke to him and to stay away from him. I decided to keep my mouth shut because I didn't want to bring more problems and not let him see his daughter. At this same time, I started having so many health problems. I lost so much weight, I wouldn't eat, and was not feeling myself. I thought it was my breakup making me feel like this, but it got more serious when I was referred to an oncologist the word cancer quickly popped into my head.

20

When you tell others you are heartbroken and he broke up with you the response I would get is "I told you so" or "He was just bored and he finally realised he was never going to have a normal life with you." Why do others blame me and my disability? All I did was truly love him with all my heart. I gave him the best of me. I saw my life with him and now I'm left empty and broken. Every single night I would cry myself to sleep and question "Why do I always end up getting fuck over?" "Why can't they choose me and want to be with me? I am emotionally and physically in pain. I had to keep going the only thing I had going for me was grad school. Even when I wanted to stay in my room and cry I pushed myself to show up to work and school. When Cristian broke up with me another of his reasons was he was going back into the military and was going to be incommuncated for three months and I believe him. Until I came across a post of his baby momma on Thanksgiving. "Oh I thought you were in boot camp," I thought out loud. I asked someone who had been in the military if someone was in boot camp can they come to visit their family and the answer was no. I had access to his phone bill his phone was active every single day and at a boot camp they take your phone away. My heart broke even more and suppose I "was" the love of his life he definitely moved on quickly. I wanted answers, but instead, I was getting more questions. You may asked if you probably hated him and the answer was no... I wanted to scream at him, but also how can I hate someone I love so much? Don't get me wrong I was so angry with him and hurt by him, but never until this day have stop loving him and I wish him the best.

I had so much going on in my personal life and to keep adding my internship workplace was so toxic. I was there for 10 months and I never received the learning and training I was supposed to. One of my coworkers would time my bathroom breaks. Yes, I took a little longer because doing everything with one hand is tricky, but there was no rule on how much time we could spend in the bathroom. This time of my life was dark. The lowest I have been ever in all aspects of my life. My health was bad, my mental health was trash, my personal life was in pieces, and grad school was kicking my ass. I was losing weight like crazy and the treatment I was put on was not helping. I would look in the mirror and I didn't recognise myself. I have no clue how I was pushing through grad school and doing A's. I got good at faking I was ill but I was dying inside. I was barely accepting the idea of never hearing about Cristian ever again. All of a sudden one night he appeared. I received a text from him and my heart dropped. I had so many emotions running through me. Since then we stayed friends and yes our romantic relationship maybe wasn't meant to be, but our friendship was. This whole story between us started as friends and he has become my best friend and I will forever cherish my friendship with him. Many people will never understand our relationship and why until this day in the present I still talk to him. I still have so many questions about why he lied and I just want the real story, but that is in the passed. Cristian will always be the love of my life. He sees me by who I am not the weird girl most people see. He supports me in my dreams and goals. He was there when I truly needed a friend. For the longest, after he reached out again I had hoped for us to get back together. I realised he wanted to be with his baby momma and not me. It might have taken me a while to accept this, but I had always wanted the best for him. If I was spiteful I could have told him how his baby momma sent her best friend Astrid to threaten me to stay away from him and all the counted messages just so they could fight. I simply didn't. I'm better than that. I didn't give in to getting down to her level. He knows he will always have a friend he can count on no matter what. I truly love him and I will always have him in my corner cheering me on. He always told me he was my number one fan and I do believe him. He is my number one supporter and hopefully, that will remain like that forever.

21

———

The last year of grad school was a real test for me. I took it upon my hands to obtain the internship placement I wanted. I saw myself working at Central Valley Regional Center before I got into grad school. I wanted to do my last year of internship there and I went for it. I reach out to CVRC and let them know my interest in doing my internship with them. I seriously thought I wasn't going to hear back from them and one day I received the call for an interview. I was so excited and nervous because this was an important opportunity and I wanted the position bad. In May 2022 I got hired at CVRC. I was on cloud nine. I felt proud of myself that I had achieved one of the professional goals I had set for myself. I was slowly building my career. I have worked so hard and I was in my last year of grad school. I could see the finishing line getting close. I had so much going on and many obstacles I thought I would never have to overcome. There were so many times I wanted to give up because I was mentally and emotionally exhausted. During this year my mental health hit rock bottom and the worst part nobody knew how badly I was struggling. In this period of my life, I saw people's true colours. I found myself so lonely, yet I pushed through showed up to classes, and worked ready to learn new things. My internship became my escape place where my mind put a pause on thinking about what was going on in my personal and focused on work. Every day at work I would always try to find ways I can better serve my clients. Showed them I was a present social worker, I listened to their needs, it was important for me to find new solutions, and most importantly was the best advocator for my clients. Working at CVRC brought me joy and fulfilment on a professional level.

Also working at CVRC gave me the purpose to show and advocate for individuals like myself that we are capable of having a professional life despite the stereotypes society has about us. What better way to utilise my social media platform? I had one million followers and I never pictured myself having that many followers. TikTok also became my escape outlet, so I decided to record my day in the office. I didn't think it would blow up as it did. Sharing my grad school journey and my work life on the Internet was one of the best decisions I have ever made. My goal with TikTok was to help bring awareness to ableism and inspire others like me that we are capable of doing anything we put our minds to. Also, without realising I was helping myself seeing how strong and hard-working of a woman I was. All the obstacles I had to push me down and I still manage to pull myself up. *Soy una chigona* I told myself how badass I was. I was unique and I was making a change in people's lives who are watching my content, society, and myself. At 30 years old

I embraced fully who I am, I love the way I was, and I didn't see my disability as a burn anymore.

In my last year of grad school had to face another obstacle. Thesis advisor, I wasn't to her liking special with the topic I chose to do my thesis on. I wanted to better the disability resources at the university campus, so future students don't have to struggle so much as I did for lack of services and information. I was told by my advisor my topic was boring and not interesting, so I had to go ahead and change my topic. I felt strongly about my topic and I stood up for myself I didn't let bullied me on changing my topic. A main part of social work is advocating and to be able to properly advocate for others, you need to start advocating for yourself first. All the discrimination and bullies I experienced I gained tough skin that finally helped me break out of my shelf. I would get messages on TikTok of individuals with disabilities and parents with children like me telling me how inspired them to go to college or gave them hope their children will have a bright future ahead. Those messages made my heart full and felt I was meant to do this and use my social media platform as a voice for not just me, but for others. With all the obstacles, ups, downs, broken heart, and health issues I got to the finish line.

On May 26, 2023, I walked across the stage and received my degree. I not only graduated, but I graduated with honours. I was so proud of myself. This achievement was for me. I was breaking stereotypes and barriers because I was part of less than one percent in the United States to obtain a master's degree with a disability. I'm being part of the change society needs. I can now utilise the tools I learned to keep being part of the change. I was meant to stand out and that's what I'm doing the best way can. Utilising my social work education via my social media has brought me so much fulfilment, and enjoyment, and helped heal my past traumas. *Soy una chigona* and empowering others via the internet showing others is okay to be different and do things differently doesn't make us less of a person.

22

At every stage of life, I always wondered why people were so surprised by the things I could do and to me, I was doing normal things everyone did. I learned society has the impression having a disability is a curse. A curse if you let it be as an individual with a disability if you accept what others tell you about how you should live your life. Then you are being part of all the stereotypes around us. All the obstacles I had to encounter I wouldn't be where I'm at now. I got asked, "If I could be born again normal, would I take the offer?" My answer was "No, Thank You." You might wonder why if when I was younger thats all I wished. Now that I'm grown and experienced all that I did I don't want to be like everyone else. The fact that I'm not "normal" actually contributed to a society that having a disability is not a bad thing. We are capable of contributing to this world in so many ways. I thank my parent for not hiding me from society like ordered families do. I always question "Why I'm always getting stared at?" now I understand is not mainly due to me moving or talking differently and more of society not being used to seeing more individuals like myself living their lives like everyone else.

Also, I see now I was meant to be the first in my classes to be there with a disability to inspire others that yes it is possible to achieve it. I love doing things differently it is what makes me to be me. The girl does her makeup with no hands just using a couch. I came to be known like this on the internet. The craziest thing after years of bullying you would think the last thing I would have done is put myself out there for strangers to bully me. The hate comments I received don't hurt me at all, instead, they make me laugh and feel bad for the person who wrote the hate comments. After being bullied for years I understood the bully was putting their insecurities on you and most likely they are unhappy with their lives. To this day is crazy to me that people who are considered "normal" feel intimidated by me. The reason is that I have a disability and I didn't let that stop me from going for my dreams. I wish I had known all this when I was younger or had someone like me around to tell me it was okay to be different. You might be asking if I would do something different. The answer is yes. I would try less of trying to fit in and care less what others thought about me because regardless they will talk about you no matter what. The Independence I have gained has given me so much confidence that I love. I enjoy doing things differently my way and to others it may seem so much work, but for me is as easy as it is for others to use their hands. I see the world differently I can keep questioning all I want of why I have to be like this, but I chose to live life to the fullest. If your dreams don't scare you, then your dreams aren't big enough. People might think I'm crazy for thinking I have a life of my own at a personal level and professionally. I always tell myself "Sí se puede" when I get a little doubt and to others "Si yo puedo, tu también puedes." If I did it you can do it too. I don't compare myself to others because that's one key to success. Everyone has their timeline. Do your race at your own pace, it might take more time, but the important is you get to the finish not when. This is a reflection of me, it might have taken me extra time, but I did it. *No me raje porque todo lo que me propongo lo logro porque soy chigona.*

I have encountered a few individuals with cerebral palsy and the cases are way more severe than mine. Many would say I'm lucky and yes I am, mostly I'm grateful. Grateful because I was allowed to voice my experience to maybe help others stop hiding because they are "different" Different is good and it is what makes you who you are. This society has built the stereotype that individuals with disabilities should kept hidden and out of the side. Guess what I broke through that barrier I'm right in the open with no shame in letting others in my life. Parents with kids with disabilities let your kids explore. Let them be who they are. Empower them to follow their dreams. Shelling them can be hard in the long run because they won't be able to defend themselves, know who they are, and most importantly be independent. Encouraging independence was key to having done the things I have achieved now. Learning how to do daily things on my own has brought me so much fulfilment in my life.

Now in the present, I feel more alive and happy where I am in my life. I'm professionally thriving and loving myself just the way I am. We all have obstacles in our lives, but I learned those obstacles make us stronger in the end. Maybe all those obstacles and experiences I had helped me become the woman I am now. I'm 31 years old the most confident I have ever been in all aspects of my life. I was born to stand out and escape the ordinary to have a positive impact on this world. Learning how to embrace fully who I am including my disability has been one of the best things. I feel without my cerebral palsy I wouldn't be who I am today. I'm successful as a social worker and as well as a social media content creator. Who would have thought the little girl who disliked putting attention on herself would be putting herself out there where millions of people see my content? Doing TikTok has boosted my confidence so much. Also, it brought my passion for properly educating others about how having a disability is not bad for society. We are capable of so much because I'm an example. I broke and kept breaking barriers to become the successful woman I dreamed of. *El querer es poder y no imposible. Soy y seguiré siendo una chingona.*

I'm ready to conquer the next chapter of my life and keep leading the path for other individuals with any type of disabilities to follow to break any barriers.